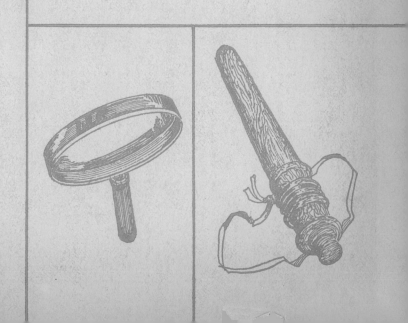

FAMOUS
INVESTIGATORS

by
Richard
Deming

illustrated by
Arnie Kohn

WHITMAN PUBLISHING COMPANY
Racine, Wisconsin

Contents

From the Very Beginning

There has been law ever since Stone Age men started to live in groups for mutual protection instead of defending themselves. The first laws, like our laws today, were based on the right of individuals to own property and to be safe from unwarranted physical attack.

Stone Age laws were very simple, of course, because life was simple. If Sheepface stole Bearwalk's stone club-ax, Bearwalk complained to the tribal council. If Bearwalk could prove his charge, Sheepface was forced to return the club-ax and was banished from the tribe for a certain period.

But police protection did not develop as early as laws. Bearwalk had no police force to call upon to solve the disappearance of his club-ax. He had to do his own detective work and gather his own evidence.

As life grew a little more complex, people began to see the desirability of appointing certain men to enforce the laws. At first these men were merely sentinels who patrolled the camps at night to prevent thievery and sound the alarm when rival bands made surprise raids. Then, as towns and cities developed, larger and better-organized police forces were necessary.

Some were quite efficient for their time. Both ancient Egypt and ancient Babylonia had not only policemen but detective forces. In the museum at Cairo there is a scrap of parchment on which a Babylonian magistrate wrote an order to a detective to arrest a certain man and *take his fingerprints*. (Fingerprinting is not as modern a device as is generally assumed. Not only was it known in ancient Babylonia, but two thousand years ago the Chinese used fingerprints for identification purposes. And the Spanish conquistadors in South

America placed thumb prints on the wax seals of treasure boxes and important letters as a means of absolute identification.)

The Greeks, an essentially law-abiding people, did not have much of a police system beyond armed patrols. The Romans, however, had a thoroughly organized police force which spanned the Empire and kept order for hundreds of years.

In the Middle Ages the science of policing suffered the same setback as all other sciences and arts. Knights and barons maintained guards to protect their own castles, and these men were supposed to protect the villages which clustered beneath castle walls as well. However, except when a village was raided by an armed force, in which case the castle guard would sally forth to defend the peasants, villagers were left pretty much to their own devices. In most villages the closest thing to a constable was the town watchman who walked the streets chanting the time— "Eleven o'clock, and all's well." If he saw a crime in progress, he yelled to awaken nearby citizens to come catch the wrongdoer. A thief did not have to be very clever to learn the watchman's schedule and arrange to commit his thievery on the opposite side of the village.

Things had not improved much by the time of the Renaissance. The night watchman, usually a lone man armed with nothing but a lantern, was still an institution in most villages. In the cities the only police protection was soldier patrols which covered such large areas that they generally hit each block only once during the night, usually at the same hour nightly. Again a criminal did not have to be very clever to avoid the patrols.

In the 1700's crime became so rampant in London that it was unsafe to walk the streets after dark except in armed groups. Pillaging of imported goods along the Thames River docks reached the point where fifty percent of the goods unloaded never reached the London merchants to which they were consigned. It was estimated that every nineteenth man in London was a criminal.

Something had to be done. In 1749, Magistrate Henry Fielding organized a police force known as the Bow Street Runners, whose duty it was to protect citizens from the thieves, footpads, and cutthroats who roamed the dark streets at night virtually unchecked.

The Bow Street Runners was not a very efficient group, but at least it constituted a police force—the first real force anywhere in the civilized world since the fall of the Roman Empire. Eventually, in 1828, this somewhat disreputable group made way for a more efficient force which today is known as Scotland Yard.

Shortly after the establishment of the Bow Street Runners, Paris also organized a police force for the same reason London had: The city was overrun by criminals. But it was not until 1812 that Paris caught up with ancient Babylonia by organizing a detective force. It started with five detectives.

Other cities followed the examples of London and Paris, and by 1800 there was some sort of police protection in most civilized communities, although much of it was quite haphazard.

Today we take an efficient, well-equipped police service for granted. If someone burglarizes our home, we pick up the phone and in a matter of minutes police are on the scene. They lift finger-prints, photograph jimmy marks, and study the M.O. (Modus Operandi, or Method of Opera-tion) of the burglar. Back at headquarters they check the prints against the local file; if there is no "make," they wire them to the Federal Bureau of Investigation in Washington. Then they go to the M.O. file where electronic sorting machines miraculously pick out from thousands of cards the records of known criminals who use a similar criminal method. An immediate roundup of these men for questioning is begun.

Perhaps the M.O. file succeeds in identifying the thief. If not, perhaps his prints prove to be on file among the 65 million sets the FBI maintains. In any event, once identified, it is only a matter of time until he is caught. If he runs from the city,

beyond the jurisdiction of the local police, he finds state police who cover the entire state. If he crosses a state line, the FBI is after him. Even if he manages to flee the country, he discovers he must contend with an organization known as Interpol which acts as a co-ordinating agency between national police forces all over the world.

Wherever he goes, the thief is hunted down by police equipped with all the modern devices of manhunting: instantaneous communications to anywhere, the finest automobiles and aircraft, modern crime labs, the best of weapons and, above all, highly skilled and thoroughly trained police officers.

These days a thief simply does not have a chance. But the police system we take for granted is a relatively recent development. You don't have to go back to the Bow Street Runners to find inadequate police service.

Even as short a time ago as the 1930's gangsters and bandits in America boldly violated the law. The average city police force was understaffed by untrained men who, in many cases, had never fired the pistols they wore. There was no co-ordination between cities, or even between states, so that criminals merely had to dodge across a jurisdictional line to be safe from pursuit. Only eleven of the forty-eight states even had state police forces, and these were primarily designed to arrest traffic violaters.

There was no nationally centralized records system until the FBI began one in 1932, and it was not until many years later that it contained the complete records it does today. If the St. Louis police, for example, wished to check the fingerprints of a suspect, they had to mail copies of his prints to a hundred or more cities, perhaps missing the single one where they were on file for some major crime. Bandits such as John Dillinger, "Pretty Boy" Floyd, "Baby Face" Nelson and others made fools of the police for years. Deadly marksmen often armed with submachine guns, they time and again blasted their way past untrained cops carrying only rusty pistols. Even when pursued, the city police could chase them only as far as the city line: state police—what few there were—had to stop at the state line. There were no effective federal law enforcement officers.

J. Edgar Hoover changed all that when he built the FBI from a politically controlled factfinding body, which did not even have the power to make an arrest, into the finest and most efficient police machine ever seen. In four years he smashed the bandit gangs, and there have been very few successful bandits since 1936.

At the same time city and state police began to examine their forces more closely. And they made drastic changes. The old days when a muscular body was the only qualification it took to get a job as a policeman are gone forever. Nowadays rookies are thoroughly examined for character, intelligence, and education, then attend police academies for rigorous training before ever donning a uniform. The modern cop can both outshoot and outthink the modern criminal.

This book commemorates some of the outstanding law enforcement officers who have made our modern system possible, either through police methods they originated or through the inspiration they passed on to others through their dedication to their jobs. Some operated in times when policing was much more difficult than it is today because of lack of modern equipment. Some are contemporary. But all occupy unique places in the history of law enforcement.

The Case of the Cat Burglar

Robert Fabian

The name Robert Fabian is as familiar to the general public in great Britain as the name J. Edgar Hoover is to Americans. Although he retired as superintendent of the Criminal Investigation Department a dozen years ago, mention of him still causes criminals to shudder. The famous Scotland Yard detective is recognized in international police circles as one of the great man hunters of the twentieth century.

As superintendent of the C.I.D., Fabian was mainly an administrator, and his solid reputation as a law enforcement officer during the latter years of his service with Scotland Yard rests largely upon the efficient way in which he organized his staff and upon the modern methods he employed. He directed many dramatic manhunts, some using hundreds of policemen, all supervised by him in their various assignments through dozens of subordinate lieutenants. But the cases he likes best to recall are those of his early years with the Yard, when he personally handled investigations on the street instead of controlling vast police efforts from a desk with half a dozen telephones. One of his favorite cases was that of the first "cat burglar."

One fall evening in 1924, a slim but well-muscled young man strolled along London's fashionable Park Lane. As was the style of the times, he wore a tailed formal jacket, black evening trousers with black satin stripes down the sides, a stiff white shirt front with a diamond stud, white bow tie, and black patent leather evening pumps. His dress was identical to that of numerous dinner guests who could be glimpsed through the windows of the elaborate Park Lane homes.

A particularly observant person might have

noticed one odd thing about the young man. The patent leather evening pumps of that period were made for dancing, with thin but hard leather soles and hard heels which would slide smoothly on waxed floors. The progress of similarly dressed men sauntering along Park Lane could be followed by the sharp clicks of their heels on the concrete sidewalk. But this man's shoes made no sound whatever.

Eight P.M. was the socially correct time to dine on Park Lane. As that hour neared the street became deserted except for an occasional formally clad guest hurrying to a dinner appointment. In the center of a block near the top of the Lane the young man paused to glance both ways along the street. Aside from a couple he had passed going in the opposite direction a quarter block back, no one was in sight.

Quickly he slipped through a gap in the hedge surrounding an elegant, old-fashioned mansion. A moment later he was crouched beneath the dining-room window.

He had timed his arrival just right, he noted with satisfaction. The Trimbles and their guests were just trooping into the dining room to sit down to dinner. For at least the next forty-five minutes they would be preoccupied with food.

Stepping back into the shadows, the young man faded toward the rear of the house. From around his waist he uncoiled a twelve-foot length of thin, black silk rope which ended in a small steel grappling hook. One expert cast upward and the hook caught the edge of a balcony drain gutter. After testing the strength of the gutter, he skittered up the rope with the effortless ease of a monkey.

On the balcony he paused to coil the rope and loop it over one shoulder where it would be instantly available again in case of emergency. Taking from his pocket a slender steel tool somewhat resembling a putty knife, he slid the blade into the slit between French windows. An instant later he was inside the second-story room.

As the clink of cutlery and the sound of gay dinner conversation drifted up from below, he unhurriedly searched every upper room. He found no cash but found several jewel boxes whose locks responded to his thin steel blade as easily as the French windows had. He took nothing but the jewels, scorning gold watches, silver cups, and other bulkier items of value.

The diners below were still absorbed in their meal when the intruder silently left the house by the same way he had entered.

Two hours later a portly, aristocratic looking man angrily entered the Vine Street police station and strode up to the desk.

"Yes, sir?" the duty officer inquired politely.

"I am Sir Wilfred Trimble," the portly man announced. "My home has just been burgled of eight thousand pounds worth of jewels." His voice became indignant. "The blasted thief had the effrontery to pilfer it while my family and a dozen guests were all in the house. I want him caught forthwith."

Sir Wilfred Trimble was only the first of a series of indignant residents of Park Lane who during the next few weeks trooped into the Vine Street station house to report jewel thefts and to demand the immediate arrest of the man the papers began to call the "cat burglar." The technique was always the same. He struck at dinner time when the aristocratic residents of Park Lane were entertaining guests in their huge dining rooms. He scaled the sheerest walls with ease, and even the strongest locks seemed to mean nothing to him. After his visits, jewel boxes were always found open and empty.

Within five weeks of the first reported theft, jewels valued at thirty thousand pounds, or nearly a hundred and fifty thousand dollars in American money, had disappeared. The duty men at the Vine Street station soon despaired whenever anyone of aristocratic bearing entered the station.

Young Robert Fabian at that time was merely a probationer fresh from a training school for detectives. He was not assigned to the case, but as the "cat burglar" was the hottest problem confronting the Vine Street station at the moment,

it was naturally a constant subject of conversation among all the officers. One crisp October
evening, Fabian and a fellow detective named
Thomas Symes were called in on extra duty to go
on a night club raid. As they sipped coffee in the
police canteen while waiting for the rest of the
raiding party, they discussed the "cat burglar."

"I've been looking the Park Lane district over
a bit in off-duty time," Symes said. "The places
he's hit so far all have a couple of things in common. The residents are all extremely rich, and the
dining rooms all have large windows surrounded
by shrubbery so that the 'cat burglar' can see
into them from concealment."

Robert Fabian grinned. "I've been doing some
off-duty work, too. Look at this."

Producing a large, folded sheet of paper
from his pocket, he spread it out before the other
detective. It was a hand-drawn map of Park Lane,
showing all the cross streets and with heavy dots
to indicate each of the hundreds of houses along
the street. A large number of the dots were circled.

"What are the circles?" Symes asked.

"Houses which meet the requirements you just mentioned. Particularly wealthy residents, and dining-room windows easily observable from concealment. Now here is where he's hit so far." He pointed out several circles on the map which had checks next to them. "He seems to be operating in a definite sequence, Tommy. First the top of Park Lane, then the bottom, then St. James. Next the top of Park Lane again, back to the bottom—"

"And next right here!" Tom Symes eagerly interrupted, suddenly seeing the sequence and pointing his finger to Arlington Street.

"Exactly," Fabian agreed. "There's also been a kind of time sequence. Six days between the first two jobs, then seven, then eight, then back to six. There haven't been enough jobs yet to say it's a definite pattern, but it could be that the next job will take place seven days after the last."

"Which is tonight," Symes said softly, gazing at his fellow probationer with respect.

In later years Robert Fabian often saw that expression of respect in the eyes of colleagues, for one of his great talents as a man hunter was his ability to put himself in the place of a wanted man and anticipate his next move. When there was a series of similar crimes, he always looked for the pattern. Maps and timetables became two of his frequently used weapons in the fight against crime.

"Do you think I ought to show this to the inspector?" Fabian asked.

Tom Symes looked doubtful. "He might think you're getting big for your boots. You aren't on the case."

There was danger of that, young Fabian knew. Probationers were supposed to follow orders, listen, and learn. They weren't supposed to give advice to veterans on how to crack cases, particularly cases to which they hadn't even been assigned. Years later, as superintendent of the C.I.D., Robert Fabian made a point of encouraging subordinates, even rookie patrolmen, to come forward with any original ideas they might have. But in this early period of his police work, probationers were to be seen and not heard.

Regretfully he folded his map and put it away. Rising to his feet, he said, "Let's go see what's holding up our call."

Together they went into the C.I.D. main room, approached the desk, and looked inquiringly at the duty inspector.

"You two still around?" the inspector asked. "That raid's off. I just announced it."

"Oh," Symes said. "We were in the canteen."

Free for the evening, the two detectives stepped outdoors. They looked at each other.

"It's only a quarter of eight," Symes said.

Fabian grinned. "Which gives us fifteen minutes to get in position."

With no further words they headed at a rapid pace for Green Park.

The Ritz Hotel was at the corner of Park Lane and Arlington Street, and Green Park was across from the Ritz. From the shrubbery in the park the detectives could see the rears of mansions for a block in each direction. But the one they concentrated on was the Wimborne house, which was circled on Fabian's map as having the requirements the "cat burglar" seemed to demand.

The dinner hour came and passed with nothing happening. After another hour, now chilled to the bone, they gave up. There was no point in waiting longer, for the "cat burglar" never struck that late.

They only quit for that evening, however. At seven thirty the next evening they were back. Tonight it was overcast enough to make it safe to approach the Wimborne house more closely. Instead of hiding in the park, the two detectives slipped over the house's garden wall and took up posts in the shadow of trees at the rear of the garden.

At eight they faintly heard a dinner gong inside the house. They strained their eyes into the darkness.

A dark figure suddenly vaulted the garden wall a dozen yards from them, landed on the grass without a sound, and disappeared into the shadows at the rear of the house. As the detectives quickly moved in that direction, they saw the figure again, this time lightly leaping from one balcony railing to another, a story above the ground.

They stared upward in amazement. Somehow the intruder had managed to run right up the side of the house faster than they were able to move on the ground.

"Get inside and raise an alarm," Fabian said in a low voice. "I'll wait here to catch him when he runs."

As Tom Symes rounded the house to the front door, Fabian flattened himself against the wall beneath the balcony where the shadowy figure had last been seen. Only a few moments passed before lights began to go on in upstairs rooms and he heard excited voices. Symes apparently had shooed everyone in the house from the dinner table to search the second floor.

There was the thudding sound of a shoulder

repeatedly being thrown against an unyielding door. It seemed to come from the room directly above, and it went on so long that Fabian began to wonder at the thief's coolness in not instantly fleeing the room before the door was broken in.

Then the "cat burglar" reappeared on the balcony beneath which Fabian crouched. Gazing upward, the detective could dimly make out that the man wore formal evening attire, including a glinting diamond stud in his shirt front.

Unhurriedly the man stepped up on the balcony railing. Fabian tensed to leap on him the moment he dropped to the ground.

But he didn't drop. With the skill of a tightrope walker he ran along the narrow iron railing of the balcony and effortlessly leaped ten feet to the next railing at the corner of the house. Fabian saw a thin, whiplike cord snake upward to a roof gutter. The figure swung out into space, landed soundlessly atop the six-foot-high garden wall, shook loose the cord, and cast it toward the roof gutter of the neighboring house. As Fabian rushed toward the garden wall, the figure swung through space again to land on a balcony railing of the second house. An instant later he was on the roof and flitting up the steeply laid tiles. Fabian caught a last glimpse of him in silhouette as he paused on the very roof peak for a moment before disappearing down the other side.

By the time the detective had scaled the garden wall and had run clear around to the far side of the neighboring house, his quarry was long gone. A phone call from the Wimborne home to the Vine Street station brought dozens of police to search the area, but the thief had made his escape.

When he finally had a moment to talk to him, Fabian asked his partner, "What was that sound of somebody trying to break down a door?"

"Me," Symes said embarrassedly. "The cool cucumber was prepared for just such an emergency. He jammed a wooden wedge under the door and went right ahead with his business while I bruised my shoulder trying to get in. I'm afraid he managed to pick up a few jewels, even after we had him cornered. That makes us look rather like idiots, doesn't it?"

"He couldn't have gotten much in that short time and from just one room," Fabian said soothingly.

But he was wrong. Jewels valued at two thousand pounds, or nearly ten thousand dollars, were missing.

The next day Fabian and Symes were given a blistering lecture by the inspector, who pointed out that if they had let him in on their plans, he could have had the place surrounded. The probationers both knew that it was more likely they would have been squelched for their presumptio in giving advice to a superior, but they made no comment.

The inspector ended by saying, "Now that you've let him escape from right under your noses, you have yourselves a case. Go and catch him."

The two detectives returned to the scene of the crime to examine it by daylight. They found a single clue. In the dust on the floor of the balcony beneath which Fabian had vainly waited for the thief to descend, there was a single, clearly defined footprint. It was so small and pointed that it looked like a woman's dancing shoe. Fabian stooped to study the print, noting with surprise that it was treaded like an automobile tire.

Rising, he said to Symes, "No wonder he moved so silently. He was wearing treaded rubber soles."

Symes raised his brows. "On patent-leather evening pumps? He'd have to get those made special."

When they returned to Vine Street to make their report, Symes was detailed to another case, which left Fabian on his own. He spent the rest of the day visiting London's exclusive shoe craftsmen where shoes were made to order. Even in a city as big as London, there weren't too many of these for only the rich had their shoes handmade.

At a place on Albemarle Street he finally found what he wanted.

"I tried to argue him out of it," the proprietor said. "Imagine evening pumps with rubber soles!

Why, you couldn't possibly dance in them because they won't slide. But that's what he insisted on, so I made them."

The record book showed that the customer had given the name R. Radd of 52 Half Moon Street and that cash had been paid for the shoes. The shoe craftsman described the purchaser as in his mid-twenties, of average height, slim, and athletic looking.

"Moved as graceful as a blooming toe dancer, he did," the shoemaker said. "I remember wondering if he might not be an acrobat."

"He is," Fabian said grimly. "But not in a circus."

The detective wasn't particularly disappointed to discover there was no 52 Half Moon Street; he had expected it to be a fake address.

To a less persistent man hunter this might have been a dead end, for the "cat burglar" seemed to have been frightened out of business by his near capture, and there were no more burglaries. But another trait of Robert Fabian's which eventually made him dreaded by all criminals was that he was incapable of giving up. And he had the patience of Job.

Reasoning that his quarry must be familiar with Half Moon Street in order to know there was no number 52, Fabian decided he either lived in that area or visited it for entertainment. At that time Half Moon Street was dotted with exclusive cafes and clubs. Evenings that he was off-duty the detective began to frequent these places, observing every man he saw and hoping to spot one matching the description given by the shoe merchant.

In those days gentlemen routinely wore evening dress after dusk on London's west side, so Fabian had to dress every night in order to remain inconspicuous. And every man he saw was dressed identically. He gazed at so many diamond shirt studs and so many pointed black pumps, his eyes began to weary.

But he kept it up, night after night for ten long nights.

On the tenth evening of his prowling from cafe to cafe he entered a place called the Range Club. The hard heels of his dress shoes clicked like drumsticks on the equally hard tile corridor.

A man passed him wearing the inevitable evening clothes and with a diamond stud sparkling in his white shirt front. At he passed, it struck the detective that his feet made no noise at all.

Glancing sidewise, Fabian saw tiny pointed shoes. Wheeling, he followed the man back out-

side. The man seemed to be somewhere in his mid-twenties, he noted, slim and of average height. And he moved with catlike grace.

There was a row of taxis outside the club, but the man with the soundless feet preferred to walk. Unobtrusively Fabian tailed him to a rooming house at 43 Half Moon Street. When the man entered it with a key, the detective was reasonably certain it was where he lived. Fabian took a taxi to New Scotland Yard.

At the Criminal Record Office they had no information about the address 43 Half Moon Street. He searched the photo files without spotting the man he had followed.

It could be coincidence, of course. His only real ground for suspecting the man he had followed was his silent footsteps, and there was no law against rubber soles. Nevertheless, the soundless shoes seemed worth investigating. When he made his report his superiors agreed with him and at once ordered twenty-four-hour surveillance of the suspect.

Two days later, while Fabian and another detective had 43 Half Moon Street staked out, the man appeared and walked to Hatton Garden, this time in ordinary street dress as it was mid-afternoon. There he met a man in a cafe, and the two took a taxi to Southgate and entered a private home.

Fabian and his colleague sat in a taxi across the street from the home for twenty minutes. Finally the man with the soundless walk came out alone. Fabian left his partner to cover the Southgate house and followed the man back to 43 Half Moon Street.

When the man disappeared inside, Fabian found a phone and called the Vine Street Station. He gave the Southgate address and asked that it be checked with the Criminal Records Office.

After a few minutes' delay the duty man reported back, "That house is occupied by a known jewel fence."

That was it, Fabian thought. He said, "I think he just made a buy. If you raid the place immediately, you should catch him with the hot goods. I left a man watching the place, so contact him before you go in. I'll stand by here at number forty-three. If you find anything at Southgate, let me know."

"Right," the duty man said and rang off.

An hour later a car pulled up across the street from number 43 and Tom Symes climbed out. Fabian stepped from the doorway where he had been lingering.

"We just pulled in that Southgate fence," Symes said with a grin. "Caught him cold with some of the jewels from the 'cat burglar' jobs. He admitted paying eight hundred pounds for them not an hour ago."

"I guess that does it," Fabian said. "Let's go."

Together the two detectives crossed the street. A middle-aged landlady answered the bell.

"We're police," Fabian said. "Do you have a roomer here about twenty-five or so, slim, well-built, and well-dressed?"

"You mean Mr. Delaney?" she asked in a

puzzled voice. "He has the upstairs flat."

The two detectives moved up the stairs. A name plate on the door of the upstairs flat read: AUGUSTUS DELANEY. The man looked up in surprise when the two detectives entered without knocking.

"Who are you?" he asked indignantly.

"Police," Fabian said. "Mind if we look over your rooms?"

The slim man paled. "What for?"

"Some jewels. And the eight hundred pounds you just received from a Southgate fence."

The "cat burglar" slowly sank into a chair. "Oh, no," he said. "I'd quit. You're not supposed to catch a man after he quits."

The eight hundred pounds was under a mattress. The remainder of the stolen jewels were concealed behind the drawer of a dresser.

Augustus Delaney received three years at Old Bailey.

Although the "cat burglar" case occurred early in Robert Fabian's career, it typified the man's

methods. In later years associates were often awed
by his ability to anticipate just what move a
criminal would make next. Fabian himself could
never understand this awe. He felt it was a policeman's duty to be able to outthink criminals, and
as he busied himself with his maps and timetables
it never occurred to him that he was doing anything remarkable. To his methodical mind,
searching out the pattern of the crime was simply
a routine procedure which any policeman should
be able to follow.

In a sense he was right, for the method he
originated is now a part of Scotland Yard routine.
But the old-timers who worked under him say that
no one ever employed it as effectively as Fabian.

When Fabian retired as superintendent of the
Criminal Investigation Division, he took up gar-
dening as a hobby. That may seem a far cry from
fighting crime, but he went at it as methodically
as he once chased criminals. His garden was always laid out in as orderly a manner as the maps
and timetables which once covered his office walls.

The Case of the Reno Roundup

Alan Pinkerton

Alan Pinkerton was the first man in the world to organize a private detective agency. John Reno was the first man in the world to organize a train robbery. The two met head on in the year 1866.

Late in the afternoon of October 6, 1866, three men boarded the wood-burning Ohio and Mississippi railroad train at Seymour, Indiana. They sat in the first coach just behind the engine.

A few miles out of Seymour the leader of the trio, a burly, dark-haired man in a rumpled blue suit, rose from his seat and moved toward the door of the second car. His companions rose, too, and followed without hurry.

44

In those days mail and money were not transported by the railroads themselves but by privately owned express companies who had their own railroad cars. These companies paid the railroads to have their cars hauled to various points, and the railroads hitched them on among their regular cars. The car the three men approached was owned by the Adams Express Company.

The express car was locked from the inside. The burly man drew a Navy Colt revolver and fired three bullets into the lock. Then he slammed open the door.

The express agent, seated at a desk in the car writing his report, looked up to be confronted by three guns. He was armed with a revolver, but he made no move for it. His arms shot up over his head.

Aside from some boxes of freight, the only cargo the express car carried was three canvas bags and an iron safe. The burly man scooped up the three canvas bags.

"Sim, you and Frank take the safe," he ordered,

and he reached up to pull the emergency brake cord.

As the train ground to a halt, the man whom the burly leader of the group had addressed as Sim rolled open the side door of the car. He and the third man rolled the safe through the door to the ground. Then the bandits jumped out.

The burly man fired his revolver in the direction of the engine. The bullet clanged against the iron boiler and whined off into the distance.

"Get that thing moving!" he yelled at the engineer.

The frightened engineer skidded the big wheels on the rails in his eagerness to get the train away.

The loot from this first train robbery in history amounted to ten thousand dollars in gold coin and thirty dollars in bills. As the robbers had not worn masks and the burly man had called his two companions by their first names, they were all quickly identified by the train crew members who had seen them. The robbers were members of the notorious Reno brothers gang. The burly man in the blue suit had been John Reno himself, the leader of the gang; the others were Simeon Reno, one of John's brothers, and Franklin Sparks, second in command of the gang.

The five Reno brothers, in order of age, were Frank, John, Simeon, Clinton, and William. All except Clinton, who was known as "Honest" Reno and had nothing to do with the rest of his family, became outlaws just after the Civil War. Many ex-soldiers turned to outlawry during this restless period, and Seymour, Indiana, was a particularly lawless community where rustlers, bandits, and cutthroats from all over the area gathered.

John Reno collected these individual outlaws into one huge band of over a hundred members and declared himself the leader. Thereafter no outlaw in that territory could commit any crime without John's personal okay beforehand and a payment of a portion of the loot afterward. With the vast sums pouring in from these criminal activities, John bribed officials, put law officers on his payroll, rigged elections in order to get his picked men in office, and eventually ruled Jackson County, Indiana, as a political dictator.

For some odd reason the Reno brothers gang has received little mention in history books compared to such outlaw brotherhoods as the James boys, the Daltons, and the Younger brothers. But in viciousness the Renos far outshadowed the other outlaw bands. They not only pulled the world's first train robbery, they organized America's first counterfeit ring, they cracked safes across five states, and they once so terrified the town of Rockford, Indiana, by systematically burning down one house after another, that the entire population of Rockford deserted the town to move to nearby Seymour. John Reno then pulled strings to make the crooked county officials pass the necessary resolutions and bought what remained of Rockford for six hundred dollars and ninety-seven cents, one of the few cases in history where an individual purchased an entire town.

After the train robbery the Adams Express Company, which bore the whole brunt of the loss,

had no trouble getting a warrant issued for the arrest of John Reno, Simeon Reno, and Franklin Sparks. But getting a warrant and serving it were two different matters in Jackson County. Every lawman in the county was on John Reno's payroll, the judges and other officials had either been elected by his crooked political machine or had been bribed into co-operation, and even among the general public a large number of residents were either kinfolk of the Renos or sympathizers. Besides that, more than a hundred armed members of the outlaw band roamed the streets of the towns in the county. Any lawman who would have dared trying to serve the warrant would have been shot on sight.

The Adams Express Company engaged Alan Pinkerton to arrest the train robbers.

Sixteen years before the train robbery, in 1850, young Pinkerton had opened the world's first private detective agency at 89 Washington Street in Chicago, Illinois. There were nine employees besides himself. Today the Pinkerton National

Detective Agency, headed by a great-grandson of the founder, employs more than three thousand people in branch offices all over the country.

Young Alan Pinkerton laid down certain rules of operation when he opened his new agency. He refused to work for rewards or, in the case of thefts or robberies, for a percentage of the recovered loot. There was a fixed daily charge plus expenses and the fee for solving a million-dollar theft was the same as for solving one of only fifty dollars. He would not touch divorce cases. He would not represent an accused criminal except with the consent of the prosecutor. He would do nothing of a shady or unethical nature, no matter what fee was offered.

Today, 113 years later, the agency operates under the same rules of integrity.

As was mentioned in the foreward, in 1850 and for a half century afterward police forces, even in the big cities, were poorly staffed, poorly trained, and generally inefficient. In some parts of the unsettled West there were no police at all, or at best untrained town marshals who were little more than hired gunmen. Consequently, Alan Pinkerton's agency was called upon for a great variety of police tasks which today would be handled by metropolitan, state, or federal police. His operatives chased and captured bandits, bank robbers, and train robbers all over the country. He broke up the Jesse James gang and jailed most of its members; he did the same with the Younger brothers gang, the Farrington gang, the Cooks gang, and the Wild Bunch. About the only famous gang of that era with whom he never tangled was the Dalton brothers, and this was only because the Daltons carefully avoided ever robbing a bank or express office which bore the sign: PROTECTED BY THE PINKERTON DETECTIVE AGENCY.

At one time or another the agency was called upon for such varied tasks as guarding a British coronation, guarding the Hope diamond, guarding the original manuscript of the Gettysburg address, and once, before the formation of the Secret Service, guarding the inauguration of a

President of the United States.

When the Adams Express Company engaged Alan Pinkerton to arrest John and Simeon Reno and Franklin Sparks, Pinkerton was a bearded man in his forties and was nationally known for the many criminal cases he had solved. The detective immediately went to Seymour, Indiana, to look over the situation.

Posing as a visiting tourist, Pinkerton wandered about the town and listened to what people had to say. If he had been recognized, he undoubtedly would never have left the town alive, but fortunately no one spotted him as the famous private detective. This was not surprising, for though Alan Pinkerton was a strongly built man, he was of only average size and had a round face with average features. Furthermore, many men wore beards at that time, so there was nothing outstanding about his appearance. Even though his name was known to everyone, he seldom was recognized on the street.

As he looked Seymour over, two things became

quickly apparent to the detective. First, there was no question about John and Simeon Reno and Franklin Sparks having actually committed the robbery, for it was common knowledge in the town; the three outlaws not only didn't bother to deny it, they even arrogantly admitted their guilt and dared anyone to do anything about it. Second, the men were so entrenched in their Seymour stronghold behind the bribed local police, crooked officials, and their army of gunmen, that it would be suicide to attempt to arrest any of them.

The only thing to do, Pinkerton decided, was to lure the three men outside of the county and arrest them on neutral ground. He quietly left town again and began to lay his plans.

A few weeks after the robbery, a pink-complexioned man with a friendly manner arrived in Seymour, rented a building, and opened a cafe. His name was Dick Winscott. The cafe served good food and quickly became popular. Among its regular customers were the Reno brothers and many members of their gang.

Dick Winscott was such an affable man that he soon became a boon companion of the Renos and their henchmen. When he hinted that he had once engaged in a little outlawry himself, the gang became even more friendly. The Renos and other gang members fell into the habit of eating all their meals at Dick Winscott's cafe and lingering to chat with the proprietor.

Before long Dick Winscott, who in reality was a Pinkerton operative, was regularly sending Alan Pinkerton information about the gang's movements and future intentions. On one occasion Winscott even managed to get John and Frank Reno to pose for a traveling photographer, and shortly afterward copies of the picture were distributed to all Pinkerton operatives.

Often word came to Alan Pinkerton that some gang member planned to visit some town outside the county. If the man were wanted somewhere or a crime were planned, Pinkerton relayed the information to the proper authorities. But never did any of the three men he was most interested in express to Dick Winscott their intention of going anywhere or doing anything.

Then, without confiding in Dick Winscott, John and Frank Reno rode across the border into Illinois, clear across that state to Missouri, and robbed the Daviess County treasury of over twenty-two thousand dollars. They were safely back in Seymour before Winscott knew they had been gone.

Since the gang was so firmly entrenched in local politics and had its own army of gunmen strolling the streets, the Missouri authorities made no attempt to go after the outlaws, even though they were thoroughly identified by witnesses who were shown the picture Winscott had smuggled to Pinkerton. But now that John Reno was wanted in another state, Alan Pinkerton decided on a change of tactics.

It seemed obvious that the three train robbers were not as loose talkers as other members of the gang and, although they all liked Dick Winscott, they were too cagey to let him know when they intended to leave the protection of Jackson County. Pinkerton decided to move into the stronghold and at least take the leader, John Reno, by force.

Pinkerton secretly sent word to Winscott instructing him to get John Reno down to the Seymour railroad station alone a few days after he received the message. He asked the operative to send him a message at Cincinnati, Ohio, as soon as he had arranged matters, giving the day and hour that the outlaw chieftain would be at the depot.

At the same time Pinkerton requested the sheriff of Daviess County, Missouri, to meet him in Cincinnati with the warrant for John Reno's arrest. Then he traveled to Cincinnati, hired six of the strongest men he could find, and rented a special two-car train. When the Missouri sheriff arrived with the warrant, Pinkerton ordered his six strong men to stay near the train constantly and sleep on it at night. He and the sheriff did the same. Steam was kept up in the locomotive day and night so that the train could take off instantly when word was received from Dick Winscott.

At last a code message came from Winscott that John Reno would be at the Seymour railroad depot the following day to meet a gang member due in on the afternoon express. Pinkerton asked for track clearance and immediately started his train westward toward Indiana.

Up until then he had not told his hired huskies what their job was to be, having merely informed them that it was a dangerous mission and if any of them wanted to back out, he should do it before the train started. Now he gathered them together for instructions.

He said, "Men, we are on our way to Seymour, Indiana, to arrest the outlaw chief, John Reno. He should be waiting for a friend at the depot when we arrive, and one of my operatives should be with him. The two of us intend to put him on this train forcibly, then continue right on through town toward Missouri. You are along to prevent any

of Reno's men who may be around from inter-
fering with the arrest. Any questions?"

"Yeah," one of the big men said dubiously.
"What if Reno's men are armed?"

"I told you there would be danger," Pinkerton
said. "Because we are serving a warrant from
another state, we don't have the authority to use
arms. Legally we should be accompanied by a
Jackson County law officer, but since they're all
in John Reno's employ, that's obviously impossible. There can be no shooting on our part, no
matter what happens. If guns are drawn against
us, it will be up to you to move fast enough to dis-
arm the men with your bare hands."

The man who had asked the question shrugged,
and the others nodded their heads in understand-
ing.

The train puffed into Seymour only minutes
before the afternoon express which John Reno
was supposed to meet. As it slowed down, Alan
Pinkerton leaned out to peer ahead at the station.
He could see Dick Winscott standing on the

platform with a large, black-haired man. Pinkerton took from his pocket the picture of John and Frank Reno which Winscott had sent him and gave it a quick glance.

"That's John Reno," he told his guards and the sheriff. "Move easy now. We want to take him by surprise."

The train wheels were still slowly turning when Pinkerton swung down to the platform. The Missouri sheriff followed, then the six powerfully built guards.

At a leisurely pace the detective approached Reno and Winscott. The others trailed after him with equal lack of hurry. There were a number of men lounging about the depot, but no one gave Pinkerton and his party more than a single, disinterested glance.

Dick Winscott looked at Alan Pinkerton with no sign of recognition when his employer stopped before him and John Reno. But as the six guards formed a silent ring about them, Reno glanced around sharply.

Pinkerton said formally, "I am Alan Pinkerton, Mr. Reno. My companion here is the sheriff of Daviess County, Missouri, with a warrant for your arrest."

Reno's right hand flashed beneath his coat, but Pinkerton knocked the gun from his hand before he could level it. The man lashed out with his left fist but the detective easily parried the blow. Then he had Reno by one arm and Winscott had him by the other. They started dragging him toward the first car of the train.

"Help!" John Reno roared. "They're kidnaping me!"

The startled depot loungers turned to stare. As it happened, none of them were members of the Reno brothers gang but a few were distant kin of the Renos. These men started to the outlaw chief's rescue, but when they saw six brawny giants standing shoulder-to-shoulder facing them, they halted and contented themselves with merely watching the drama.

Pinkerton and Winscott managed to get the

struggling outlaw on the train. Tripping him, they held him flat on his face while the sheriff snapped on handcuffs behind his back. Then Pinkerton waved to the engineer, and the train began to chug out of the station and on toward Illinois. The six guards swung aboard as it began to move.

The whole battle was not yet won, however. The depot loungers lost no time in reporting John Reno's capture to his brothers. The brothers quickly gathered together as many gang members as they could on such short notice and started in pursuit.

Horses could run faster than trains in those days, but only for short stretches. Coming to a siding where a railroad train was parked, the gang took over the train at gunpoint. The fleeing Pinkerton train roared across the Illinois border and on toward Missouri with the outlaw train in hot pursuit.

But the gang never caught up. At the Missouri border the outlaws were so far behind that they abandoned the chase, turned the stolen train around, and headed back home.

Alan Pinkerton's train triumphantly chugged into Gallatin, Missouri, where John Reno was placed in jail. Later convicted of robbery, he was sentenced to the state penitentiary at Jefferson City, Missouri, for twenty-five years.

The warrants for the Adams Express car robbery were never served on Simeon Reno and Franklin Sparks. But as the gang, now headed by Frank Reno, continued on its course of robbery and burglary, eventually Alan Pinkerton arrested the remaining two outlaw brothers, and a dozen other members of the gang, for other crimes.

Bereft of leadership, the remaining gang members gradually drifted away from Seymour to areas where things weren't quite so hot, and law and order once more returned to Jackson County.

The Reno case illustrates Alan Pinkerton's outstanding characteristic: absolute refusal to give up. After the police of two states had shown unwillingness to brave John Reno's stronghold, one might think that a mere private detective would be daunted. But it never occurred to Pinkerton to refuse the assignment. He tried one plan to get Reno; when that failed he personally plunged right into the stronghold and took the bandit chieftain by force. If the second plan had failed, he would have come up with a third, fourth, fifth, or hundredth. From the moment the Adams Express Company turned the matter over to him, John Reno was doomed to prison. Sometimes it took him years, but Alan Pinkerton did not fail to get his man.

This bulldog tenacity earned him such respect among lawbreakers that many went to great pains to insure that he never got on their trails. The Dalton brothers gang was the first major outlaw band of that period to follow the sensible procedure of never robbing a bank or express company protected by the Pinkerton Agency, and with later gangs it became axiomatic that you did nothing to set Pinkerton on your trail.

Prison was too certain for any outlaw who made that mistake.

The Case of the Missing Jewels

Raymond Schindler

If Alan Pinkerton had the distinction of being the world's first private detective, the late Raymond Schindler has the distinction of raising the art of criminal detection to its present high scientific level. He was the most famous private investigator of modern times.

The modern private detective agency, like the modern police force, has many advanced tools which were unknown in Alan Pinkerton's day. The Schindler Bureau of Investigation, still in operation as one of the country's major private detective agencies, although its founder died a few years ago, employs fingerprint experts, handwriting experts, crime laboratory technicians, lie detector operators, even a physicist. Many of Schindler's most widely publicized cases were solved through the use of highly technical scientific methods that more closely resembled scientific research than criminal investigation.

But even in this complicated modern world, there are times when all the scientific tools of crime detection are of no avail and the investigator must fall back on plain, old-fashioned reasoning. Ray Schindler was famous for his scientific methods, but he was also as great a deductive genius as the fictional Sherlock Holmes. One of his most interesting cases was solved almost wholly by his brilliant reasoning without the use of any scientific gadgets at all.

The affair began on a warm Tuesday morning at the Brooklyn home of Mr. and Mrs. Gerald Bailey.* The Baileys were moderately wealthy and Mrs. Bailey owned a jewel collection, given her by her husband, which was valued at fifty

*All names except Raymond Schindler's are fictitious, though the case is true.

thousand dollars. She regularly cleaned her jewels every six months, and today a cleaning was due.

The jewelry, which consisted of rings, bracelets, necklaces, earrings, and pins set with diamonds and emeralds, was first washed with soap and water, rinsed in a solution of vinegar water to cut the soap, then dipped in alcohol to give it sparkle. When this ritual was completed, Elizabeth Bailey spread a bath towel across the top of her dressing table and placed the jewelry on it to dry. Then she went downstairs to do her housework.

An hour later Elizabeth went back upstairs to put the jewel collection away. The towel was completely bare.

There was no one else in the house but a German cook named Emma Lischer. Rushing down the back stairs into the kitchen, Elizabeth cried, "Emma, all my jewels are gone!"

"*Nein!*" Emma exclaimed.

The two women went back upstairs together and helplessly stared at the bare towel. The stolid cook was the first one to calm down enough to have an idea.

"Better you should phone the mister," she advised.

A phone call to his office brought Gerald Bailey hurrying home. He, his wife, and Emma searched the house from top to bottom without finding the gems.

"Who was here today?" Gerald Bailey asked.

"No one," Elizabeth said. "Except the postman, of course. But he couldn't have gotten in, because the front door was locked. I remember unbolting it to get the mail, and I locked it again when I came inside."

Bailey looked at the cook. "Did anyone come in the back way, Emma?"

"Just the grocery boy. But he was not my sight out of. He leave his groceries and go."

Gerald Bailey telephoned the police, then his insurance agent. The jewels were insured for four-fifths of their value, and forty thousand dollars is a large amount for an insurance company to pay.

The insurance agent arrived before the police did.

When the police arrived the first thing they did after questioning Elizabeth and Emma was make a study of the premises. Although it was warm enough for windows to be open, they all contained screens locked from the inside, and none had been cut. Elizabeth Bailey's insistence that the front door had not been unlocked for a moment, except when she stepped outside for the mail, ruled out the possibility of a sneak thief having entered that way. The only other way into the house was by the back door, and Emma testified that she had not been out of the kitchen for a minute and that the only visitor had been the grocery boy.

"He was never my sight out of," she added.

Next the police, assisted by the insurance man, thoroughly searched the house, with no more success than the Baileys and Emma had had. The police seemed to suspect it was an inside job, which divided suspicion between Emma and Elizabeth. But if either had stolen the gems, how had they taken the jewels out of the house? Both women swore the other had been indoors all morning.

It was possible, of course, that either might have slipped outside for a moment without the other knowing. The outside grounds were searched as thoroughly as the house had been, again without success.

The police gave up. The worried insurance agent phoned Raymond Schindler to solve the case.

When the detective arrived in response to the insurance man's frantic plea for haste, the police had already departed, Gerald Bailey had returned to his office, and no one was there but Elizabeth, Emma, and the insurance man. The latter, breathing a sigh of relief that the matter was now in the competent hands of the famous detective, introduced Schindler to Elizabeth Bailey and then hurried off on other business.

Schindler studied the tearful Elizabeth Bailey as she repeated the story she had already told to Emma, then to her husband, then to the insurance man and, finally, to the police. She was a dark, beautiful woman, he noted, but highly nervous. Her hands worked together constantly and occasionally her whole body trembled. It was natural for her to be upset over the loss of her jewels, he thought, but since they were largely insured it seemed to him she was taking it unusually hard.

After hearing both Elizabeth's and the cook's stories, the detective looked over the house. It was an old-fashioned building full of ornate, carved furniture and hanging bird cages containing singing canaries and squawking parakeets. In addition cats wandered all about the rooms, and there was a pet monkey who leaped from chair to chair, ran up and down the draperies and periodically practiced gymnastics on the chandeliers.

"You must be fond of pets," Schindler commented politely.

"We haven't any children," Elizabeth said in a sad voice. "Our pets sort of take the place of them." Then she brightened. "Ming is almost like a child to us. Isn't he cute? Ming, say hello to Mr. Schindler."

The monkey, at the moment perched atop a huge enameled Chinese vase three feet tall, cocked his head when the woman spoke to him as though he understood every word she said. Apparently he did, for he leaped from the vase to his mistress's shoulder, gravely bobbed his head at the detective, and chattered a string of monkey talk.

Amused, the detective said with a grin, "Glad to meet you, Ming."

Schindler's tour of the house confirmed what the police had already decided: No sneak thief could have gained entry and stolen the gems. With Mrs. Bailey's permission he searched the whole house and the outside grounds, although he knew the police had already done this. He had a healthy respect for the thoroughness of the police, but he still preferred to see things for himself.

The search failed to turn up any jewels.

It seemed to the detective that there could be but one logical solution to the mystery. Either Emma or Elizabeth Bailey herself was guilty of

the theft. And since neither had left the house, there must have been an accomplice who came either to the front or back door and was handed the jewels.

The only persons known to have visited the house that day were the grocery boy and the mailman; the first order of business was, then, to investigate them. Phoning his office, Schindler arranged for several operatives to look into their backgrounds. He also left instructions for additional operatives to question all of the Bailey's neighbors to find out if any callers had been seen going to either the front or back door.

The mailman, who was near retirement age, had been on the same route for fifteen years and was given the highest character rating by his branch postmaster. It seemed inconceivable that he would conspire with a jewel thief. It was possible he had been used unknowingly, however. The operative asked him if anyone at the Bailey house had given him a package to mail that day.

The mailman said no.

The grocery boy also was rated high in character and honesty by his employer, and it seemed
equally unlikely that he would act as accomplice
to a thief.

The operatives who questioned neighbors
found one who had seen the mailman deliver the
mail and another who had seen the grocery boy
enter and leave by the back door. The former was
sure the mailman had merely dropped the mail in
the box and had gone on without going to the
front door or speaking to anyone from the house.
The latter had noted nothing suspicious in the
grocery boy's actions.

No one in the neighborhood could recall seeing
any other visitors to the Bailey home that morning.

Up to this point the investigation had taken two
days. On the next day Ray Schindler and one of
his operatives divided the neighborhood into two
parts and began visiting every business establishment within a half mile of the Bailey home. At
each place they asked if on the morning of the

jewel theft any delivery had been made to the Bailey home.

It was Schindler who hit the jackpot. Entering a telegraph office, he repeated the same question he had asked in dozens of other places.

"Mrs. Bailey?" the manager said thoughtfully. "That name's familiar. Just a minute while I look at last Tuesday's log."

After flipping through a record book, he said, "Yes, here it is. Are you a police officer?"

"Private," Schindler said, showing his identification. Despite the actions of some fictional detectives, it is a rule of all reputable private agencies that an operative must never pose as a police officer in order to gain information.

The manager, recognizing Schindler's name, was more impressed than if he had been the chief of police. He said, "I'm sure it will be all right to give you the information, Mr. Schindler. Mrs. Bailey telephoned for a messenger boy last Tuesday morning. She had him take a package to the post office and send it by registered mail to an address in Kansas City. Would you like the address?"

"I certainly would," the detective said fervently.

The manager read off the address, and the detective wrote it down. The package had been mailed to a woman.

No wonder Mrs. Elizabeth Bailey had seemed so nervous, Schindler thought. On the very morning of the jewel theft she had mailed a registered package and had neglected to mention it to her husband, the police, her insurance agent, or himself.

Returning to his office, he phoned a private detective in Kansas City with whom he had a working agreement and asked him to investigate the addressee of the package and see if he could learn what its contents had been. Then he sat back to wait.

The Kansas City detective phoned back the next day.

"I've got the dope, Ray," he said. "The woman

is just a cover address for her boy friend, a shady character named Henry Bullock. He's an ex-con. I threw a scare into her and got her to tell me the whole story. There were five hundred dollars in small bills in the package, not jewels. Seems regularly every six months Mrs. Bailey mails a similar wad to be relayed on to Bullock. The girl claims she doesn't know what the money is for, but it sounds to me like blackmail."

"Thanks," Schindler said. "Mail me a bill for your service."

He was a little disappointed when he hung up. He had thought the mystery of the disappearing jewels was solved, but all that had developed was another mystery.

Then it occurred to him that perhaps the blackmail payments, if that's what they were, were the answer to what had happened to the jewels. Perhaps Elizabeth Bailey had been selling them a bit at a time in order to meet the blackmail demands and finally, when the last piece was gone, had reported them stolen. There was no verification for her story that she had left them drying on her dressing table. They might have been missing for weeks or even months.

He decided to return to Brooklyn and confront Mrs. Bailey with what he had learned. Perhaps the knowledge that he knew she was paying blackmail would jolt a confession from her.

The beautiful Elizabeth Bailey seemed apprehensive when she saw who had come to call. Again it struck Ray Schindler that her reaction to the jewel theft was too strong for a totally innocent person.

As she showed him into the front room a cat rubbed against either leg. Canaries in four different cages were singing enthusiastically, and a parakeet in another cage squawked, "Hello, hello, hello." Ming came racing from the next room to perch on the mantel and chatter a greeting.

Over the uproar Schindler said, "I just received a phone call from an associate of mine in Kansas City, Mrs. Bailey."

The woman turned white. Sinking onto the

sofa, she said in a faint voice, "Concerning what, Mr. Schindler?"

"Concerning the money you have been mailing to Henry Bullock every six months."

Elizabeth began to tremble and then to cry. The monkey leaped from the mantel to the sofa, anxiously looked up into her face, and began to pat her arm.

Real-life private detectives are seldom as tough and hard-natured as those of fiction. Ray Schindler happened to be a particularly soft-hearted man who couldn't stand to see a woman cry. His stern manner evaporated, and he found himself trying to soothe the woman.

"Perhaps if you told me about it, I could help you," he suggested.

This only brought on more tears. "It will all come out," she sobbed. "My husband will leave me."

"If the blackmail payments have any bearing on the jewel theft, I'll have to inform the insurance company," the detective admitted. "But if you satisfy me that they don't, there's no reason anyone else has to know your secret."

Wiping her eyes with a tiny handkerchief, the woman looked up beseechingly. "I swear it has nothing to do with the jewels, Mr. Schindler. I have no idea what happened to them."

"Then tell me about Kansas City."

With a resigned sigh, she said, "I suppose I have no choice. I'll tell you the whole story."

She said that as a young girl in a small Missouri town she had worked as a bookkeeper in a bank. She fell in love with and became engaged to a young bank teller. Unknown to her, many of the bookkeeping entries he gave her were false, and because she loved and trusted him, she entered them without question.

Then one day they were both arrested. He was tried for embezzlement, convicted, and sent to the state penitentiary at Jefferson City. She was tried as his accomplice but was acquitted.

Later she came to New York, got a job as a secretary, and eventually married her husband. For three years she was sublimely happy, for they loved each other deeply. The only flaw in her happiness was her dread that someday her husband might learn she had once been on trial for embezzlement. Although she had been acquitted, it had been merely for lack of evidence, and she knew that in the small Missouri town a stigma of guilt still hung over her head. Her husband was an extremely religious and honest man, and she was sure he would leave her if he ever heard of her indiscretion.

Finally what she feared happened. A man called on her when her husband was not at home, introduced himself as Henry Bullock, and said he had been a cell mate of her former fiancé. He knew all about her past trouble and threatened to tell her husband if she didn't comply with his demands. He said he wasn't greedy and would settle for five hundred dollars every six months, to be mailed in small bills to his girl friend in Kansas City.

"I've been paying ever since," she concluded

wearily. "My husband is a very generous man and never questions my expenditures, so he never suspected."

As she spoke her tears had stopped, and the monkey lost his anxiety. Snuggling into her arms, he began to toy with the bright buttons of her dress, attempting to pull them loose. Absently she kept brushing his little hands away.

Schindler suddenly had an idea. Taking a small silver pencil from his pocket, he began twisting it in his fingers so that the sunlight streaming through a window glinted from it. The monkey was attracted by this new toy and lost interest in the little buttons.

"You should never have agreed to the payments," the detective said. "There is only one way to deal with a blackmailer. You should have marched to the phone and asked for the police the moment you learned what he wanted."

"But then the whole story would have come out," she protested.

Schindler shook his head. "Bullock would

never have waited for the desk sergeant to answer the phone. He would have been out the door the minute you asked for the police, and you would never have heard from him again." Casually laying the silver pencil on an end table, he said, "Would you step into the next room with me for a minute, Mrs. Bailey?"

Giving him a bewildered look, she rose to her feet. "All right. But why?"

"I want to show you something," he said, escorting her to the door.

The moment they were outside the room, Schindler turned and looked back. The monkey had leaped to the end table and was grasping the bright silver pencil. As he scampered toward an opposite door, the detective hurried after him. Her bewilderment now giving way to complete astonishment, Elizabeth followed the detective.

They reached the doorway through which the monkey had disappeared to find him perched atop the big enameled Chinese vase. The pencil was nowhere in sight.

As Schindler approached the vase the monkey bared his teeth and hissed at him.

"Why, you naughty Ming!" Elizabeth said, rushing forward to scoop him into her arms. "You know you like Mr. Schindler."

"Don't blame him," Schindler said. "He doesn't like the fact that I've discovered his hiding place."

Whereupon he bent to peer into the narrow mouth of the vase. The opening was too small and it was too dark inside to see anything.

With effort he tipped it over and gently laid it on its side. Three feet tall and about two feet wide, it was very heavy. Grasping the base, he tipped it to nearly a ninety degree angle, the mouth downward.

The first thing to roll out was his silver pencil. There followed a stream of small coins, buttons, and other bright objects. Then there cascaded out a whole stream of glittering jewelry.

"My jewels!" Elizabeth cried, kneeling to retrieve them. "Ming, you naughty little kleptomaniac!"

"I guess the case of the missing jewels is solved," Schindler said. "I'll make a report to the police and the insurance company. I'll also take care of the blackmailer for you. Just stop sending him money and forget about him."

Rising to her feet with the jewels clasped to her bosom, she gazed at him with tears in her eyes. "How wonderful you are, Mr. Schindler! But how will you do it?"

"Don't worry," the detective said dryly. "I know how to deal with blackmailers. You'll never hear from him again."

Returning to the office with the woman's heartfelt thanks still ringing in his ears, he phoned Kansas City again.

"I need another favor," he told his detective friend. "I want you to go back to that woman and ask how to find Henry Bullock. When she asks why, tell her you have a warrant for his arrest. Say that Mrs. Bailey tired of paying blackmail and confessed to her husband. He forgave her but wants the blackmailer arrested and sent to jail. Have you got all that?"

"I've got it," the Kansas City man said. "She won't tell me where to find Bullock, of course. But she'll relay what I say on to him. And Henry will scoot for parts unknown."

"You get the pitch," Schindler said. "Thanks a lot."

Henry Bullock was never heard from again— at least, by Elizabeth Bailey.

At the time of the Bailey case Raymond Schindler was well-known in New York, but he had not yet gained the worldwide reputation he eventually earned. He first made international headlines in 1943 by his masterful scientific investigation of the sensational death of Sir Harry Oakes in the Bahamas. Engaged by the defense attorneys of the accused Alfred De Marigny, he established the man's innocence through irrefutable scientific means in one of the most logical and orderly presentations of evidence ever rendered in a courtroom.

Later he again received worldwide attention

as a member of the Erle Stanley Gardner team which came to be known as "The Court of Last Resort." This group originated when lawyer and mystery-writer Gardner discovered an innocent man in prison and set about to have him freed by the courts. Realizing that there must be many similar innocent persons wrongly convicted of crimes they did not commit, Gardner organized a volunteer group to investigate such cases. Wanting only top men, he gathered about him the world's foremost authority on medical jurisprudence, the world's top crime lab technician, and the world's foremost lie detector operator. To round out the group, it was only natural that he chose the world's most famous private detective. For a number of years Schindler contributed his efforts to this project and was instrumental in freeing many innocent persons from prison, in some cases years after their wrongful convictions.

Ray Schindler's real-life accomplishments far outshine anything that fictional private eyes have been able to accomplish in mystery books.

The Fontaine Case

François-Eugéne Vidocq

The law enforcement officers in this book have been picked because of particular contributions to the war against crime. Some stand out above the crowd because of their advanced methods, others for their deductive talents, and still others for their organizing ability. Of them all, however, only François-Eugéne Vidocq has a double distinction.

You would think that founding and serving as the first commissioner of the famous Sûreté Nationale of France would be enough to insure him a solid place in the history of law enforcement. But Vidocq was not only the most famous detective of his day. He was, prior to his reformation and entry into police work, the most notorious criminal in France.

A brilliant man, Vidocq didn't make the mistake of concentrating on a single type of crime as most criminals do. The average thief who once successfully cracks a safe, usually continues cracking safe after safe until he is finally caught. The average confidence man uses the same gimmick over and over until he, too, is caught. Every police force has an M.O. (*Modus Operandi*) file describing the particular techniques of known criminals, and many thieves are caught simply because they haven't the foresight to vary their techniques. Vidocq ran the whole gamut of crime. He was a master confidence man, a counterfeiter, a smuggler, a jewel thief, and a highwayman. In the early 1800's this master criminal had the Paris police reeling in circles.

Nevertheless Vidocq's criminal career proves that in the end crime simply can't pay. Although probably one of the most brilliant criminals in history, eventually he was caught and sentenced to serve eight years in prison.

At this point M. Henry, chief of the Paris Préfecture, made a unique decision. Chances were that Vidocq would be freed in about five years, or perhaps even escape sooner, and the police would have to track him down all over again. The chief set out to remove him as a source of future embarrassment to the Préfecture by reforming him.

With the ordinary criminal such an approach would be doomed to failure, M. Henry knew, but Vidocq was no ordinary man. He was not only brilliant but had a high code of honor, despite his criminal activities. Henry had long suspected that Vidocq's primary interest in crime was not financial gain but merely the pleasure he got from confounding the police. Vidocq regarded it as a game of wits. Henry reasoned that if he could lure him to the other side of the law, he would make as brilliant a policeman as he had a criminal.

Accordingly Henry submitted to Vidocq the proposition that he would use his influence to obtain a pardon, providing the master criminal would agree to forego his life of crime and thereafter work on the side of law and order. No doubt the promise of a pardon had some effect on Vidocq's acceptance of the offer, but it was also likely that the game of outwitting the police was beginning to pall, and the new game of pitting his skill against the underworld appealed to him. At any rate all Paris was confounded when it was announced that the notorious François-Eugéne Vidocq had not only been pardoned but had been appointed a policeman.

M. Henry's remarkable action soon proved the wisest police move he ever made, for it instantly accomplished two things. Vidocq never again committed an illegal act, which removed a large thorn from the side of the police, and he proved to be the most brilliant detective of his day. One of his first actions was the capture of the murderous Fossard gang which had been terrorizing Paris for years. And as success followed success, the Parisians lost their uneasiness over having a former criminal assigned to protect their lives and property, and they began to follow his remarkable feats of crime detection with as close an interest as they formerly had followed his duels of wit with the police.

Vidocq was a natural detective, for he had such powers of deduction that no ordinary criminal was a match for him. His reputation became so great that criminals, figuring it was a hopeless contest, often turned themselves in when they learned that Vidocq was on their trail; since he would inevitably snare them in the end, they might as well surrender and hope for leniency.

In 1812 the chief of the Paris Préfecture decided to form a detective force and detailed Vidocq to establish it. Vidocq asked for four picked assistants and called his new bureau the Brigade de Sûreté. By 1817 the Sûreté had grown to thirteen members and was already famous as a detective force. Today the body, now employing hundreds, is known as the Sûreté Nationale and ranks in international reputation with such world-famous police organizations as Scotland Yard, the FBI, and the Royal Canadian Mounted Police.

It is difficult to pick a typical Vidocq case because the man brought to police work the same versatility he had practiced as a criminal. He rarely used the same approach to a solution of a crime more than once. His methods varied so enormously from case to case that it was impossible for criminals even to begin to predict what he might do. But perhaps the Fontaine case is as representative as any.

Jules Fontaine was a butcher in the town of Courtille. One summer day in 1827 he started to walk from Courtille to a fair in the Corbeil district. He expected the walk to take him a full twenty-four hours, but the length of the journey was not unusual. For those who didn't own horses and didn't care to spend money on public stage coaches, their feet furnished the only transportation available. People often walked fifty or a hundred miles.

Intending to buy some cattle at the fair, Fontaine carried fifteen hundred francs in his pocket. As dusk began to fall, he reached an inn near Essonnes and decided to stop for dinner.

There were several tables at the inn, but only one was occupied. Two tall, well-dressed men sat at it.

It was the friendly custom in those days for wayfarers who met at inns to join each other for dinner, even if they were total strangers. As Fontaine entered the two men smiled in his direction.

The taller, darker man said, "Good evening, *monsieur*. We have just ordered dinner, if you'd like to join us."

Setting his walking staff in a corner, the butcher seated himself at the table. "I'm Jules Fontaine," he announced.

The two men introduced themselves as M. Du Bois and M. Berré, merchants en route to Millay. The butcher informed them that he himself was on the way to the fair to buy cattle.

"You don't plan to go on tonight, do you?" M. DuBois asked with raised brows. "The roads are infested with highwaymen."

Fontaine laughed and pointed to his walking staff. "I think I could manage any highwayman."

The butcher was a huge man with thick arms and a burly chest. After examining his frame, DuBois nodded. "I guess you could put up a good fight," he agreed.

The men were such pleasant companions that the butcher lingered over his meal. It was quite dark when he finally rose to go on.

"Sure you ought to risk the road in the dark?" DuBois asked.

"I want to be at the fair early in the morning, before all the best stock is gone."

DuBois looked at his companion. "Why don't we go on tonight, too, then, M. Berré? The three of us should be able to handle even a band of highwaymen."

Berré agreed to this, and the three men left the inn together. Companionably they trudged through Essonnes and on toward Millay. A few miles beyond Essonnes they came to a small lane between high hedges which forked off the main road.

"This is a short-cut to Millay," DuBois said. "It'll save several miles."

Agreeably Jules Fontaine turned into the lane with his two companions. It was narrower than the main road, allowing room only for two men abreast. The butcher and Berré walked ahead, DuBois falling in behind them.

Without warning the butcher suddenly felt a terrific blow on the back of his head. He was wearing a thick woolen cap and also had thick hair, but the force of the blow drove him to his knees. The man who had been walking alongside him brought his walking staff down across his back, driving him flat on his face.

The butcher was a powerful man, though. From his prone position he lashed out with his own stick and managed to catch the ankles of one of his assailants. With a howl of pain the man stumbled back. The next instant Fontaine was on his feet, swinging his staff at the second man.

The initial blow from behind had partially stunned him, however, and in his groggy state he was no match for a pair of footpads who were experts at fighting with staves. Fontaine managed several telling blows, but the robbers delivered more. Gradually he was beaten into insensibility.

When the butcher awoke it was broad daylight. His pockets no longer held the fifteen hundred francs.

There had been some twenty similar robberies in that area in recent months, and the local police had been considering for some time asking for the assistance of the Sûreté. This latest outrage was the determining factor. An official request to investigate the robbery was sent to Vidocq.

The detective's first step was to visit the victim, who was recovering from his beating in a hospital at Millay. He got little information that he didn't already know except some rather vague descriptions of his assailants. The butcher described them both as tall, well-built men who were exceedingly well-dressed, but he could recall no distinctive

features or mannerisms. He did remember that the smaller of the two had a rather peculiar walk. It wasn't quite a limp, he said, but a tendency to drag his feet in a kind of shuffle.

Vidocq next visited the inn where the victim had met the robbers. The innkeeper remembered the men but claimed he had never seen them before and could give no better descriptions than the butcher had. He said he hadn't noticed the distinctive gait of the smaller man.

With an assistant the detective then visited the scene of the crime. Evidence of the terrific struggle the butcher had given was still there. The dirt of the lane was churned up by heavy footprints, several of them still remarkably clear impressions.

Vidocq was one of the earliest of scientific detectives. That day he used a technique which most modern police forces still use today: He preserved the footprints by making plaster casts of them. Then he sent his assistant back to the hospital with the casts to compare them to the shoes of the victim. After eliminating the prints which had been made by the butcher's feet, he now had casts of the footprints of both robbers.

In those days shoes were handmade by cobblers, not turned out by machine in identical pattern by the thousands. While there was nothing distinctive about either set of prints, Vidocq knew that only one pair of shoes in all the world would exactly fit each set.

While his assistant was at the hospital, Vidocq continued his examination of the scene of struggle. He found a pair of buttons which had been torn from the coat of one of the highwaymen. Widening his search of the area to include the tall grass edging the lane, he eventually turned up a small scrap of paper.

The scrap seemed to be part of the cover sheet of some kind of legal document, possibly a summons or a tax bill. The sheet had been torn right across the middle. Vidocq assumed that the document must have been protruding from the pocket of one of the robbers, and a lucky blow of the butcher's staff had ripped loose this tiny but possibly important scrap. It read:

> *Monsieur* Rao——
> *Marchand di Vins*, bar——
> Roche——
> Cli——

The detective felt sure the words represented the name and address of one of the robbers, and if he could fill in the part which had been torn away, he would know at least one of the thugs. Returning to his Paris office, he laid the scrap on his desk and carefully studied it.

The first line was obviously the man's name, but thousands of French names began with the letters Rao——. Furthermore, it was impossible to tell if it were the beginning of a first or a last name, as the custom of the time made it proper to address letters and documents either with the full name or with only the last.

The second line offered a little more. *"Marchand di Vins"* meant "Merchant of Wines," so

Vidocq knew his quarry operated a wine shop somewhere. The last two lines seemed to be part of the address of the wine shop.

From this meager data Vidocq proceeded to perform one of the most remarkable deductive feats in the history of criminology. Today a police officer with the information Vidocq had could go to an electronic sorting machine, press a few buttons, and automatically the machine would produce a stack of punch cards bearing the names of all known criminals who operated, or ever had operated, a wine shop. But in 1827 police records were scanty. The Sûreté had no such file.

Furthermore, operating a wine shop was a common front for many criminals in the France of that day. There were literally thousands of wine merchants throughout France who had been afoul of the law at some time or other.

Although he lacked adequate files to refer to, François-Eugéne Vidocq had a vast knowledge of the underworld, both from his early days as a part of it and from his later police work. He had a mental file of thousands of criminals, their names, habits, and various fronts, all neatly charted in the recesses of his memory.

Mentally sorting through this huge file, he dredged up the name of every criminal he could think of who had ever operated a wine shop. Hour after hour he stared at the wall, examining names from his memory and discarding them.

Finally the name Jean Raoul popped into his mind. This wine merchant had no police record but had once been suspected of smuggling, and this was enough for him to have found a place in the detective's mental file.

Checking the address of M. Jean Raoul's wine shop, Vidocq found that it matched the scribbling on the scrap of paper. Reconstructed in full, the writing said:

Monsieur Raoul
Marchand di Vins, barriére
Rochechouart *chaussée de*
Clignancourt

Now that he knew the identity of one of the robbers, he set out to discover the other. He detailed several detectives to watch the shop and others to make inquiries among neighbors.

The detectives watching the shop reported that one tall, well-dressed man seemed to be a particular crony of Raoul's. He spent many hours in the wine shop, and he seemed to be well supplied with funds.

Other detectives, moving about the neighborhood, heard whispers that Raoul and his friend often disappeared for days at a time, always returning marked with the stains of long travel and with their pockets full of francs.

Vidocq liked to see things for himself. Stationing himself across from the wine shop with one of the detectives who was watching the place, he patiently waited for hours until M. Raoul's friend finally appeared. As soon as his assistant pointed out the man, Vidocq recognized him as a criminal he had arrested years before on a charge of robbery with violence. His name was Georges Court.

The man had a peculiar walk. It was not a limp but a sort of shuffling motion caused by dragging his feet.

Vidocq patiently waited more hours until Georges Court finally emerged from the shop. Following him home, the detective learned that he lived in an apartment on the Rue Coquenard.

Returning to his office, Vidocq obtained a warrant for the arrest of Georges Court. But as he had not yet a shred of evidence to tie the man to the robbery of Jules Fontaine, he didn't have the warrant made out for robbery. French law required that a charge be placed within twenty-four hours of arrest, or else the suspect must be released. Vidocq had no intention of tipping his hand too soon and permitting the robbers to escape justice through a technicality. He therefore had the warrant made out for the relatively minor offense of smuggling.

Vidocq went to the apartment on Rue Coquenard to serve the warrant personally. When Court recognized the famous detective he turned deathly pale. But when he discovered his arrest was only on suspicion of smuggling, he smiled in relief. He made no objection to being dragged off to police headquarters.

While other detectives kept Court busy answering questions about his alleged smuggling operations, Vidocq thoroughly searched the apartment. In a closet he found a coat with two missing buttons, and the remaining buttons matched the ones he had located at the scene of Jules Fontaine's beating and robbery. There was also a pair of heavy walking boots which matched one of the casts of footprints made at the scene of the crime. And, finally, he turned up a cache of pistols and daggers.

This was enough at least to place a charge against Georges Court, but first Vidocq wanted evidence against his fellow robber. He decided to visit the wine shop of Jean Raoul.

Again the detective didn't want to tip his hand and risk having Raoul slip through his fingers.

If he could trap the wine merchant into voluntarily allowing him to search his shop and the rooms above it, he might be able to uncover the evidence he needed without the legal necessity of having to place a charge against the man in twenty-four hours.

Accordingly he greeted Raoul affably when he entered the wine shop. The proprietor recognized him at once and was immediately on guard. The detective was carrying a small attache case, and Raoul eyed it suspiciously.

"I have a complaint that you've been holding meetings in your apartment upstairs," Vidocq told the man.

"You mean the card games I sometimes hold?" Raoul asked in surprise. "There's no law against a man playing cards in his own house."

"I thought it would turn out to be something like that," Vidocq said with an amiable smile. "You know how jittery the government is these days. They imagine a revolution is being planned every time a group gets together to play a little

cards. This sort of thing is really a political matter instead of a police matter, but I've been
ordered to check up, so I have to do it."

Raoul smiled with relief. It was true that the
government was jittery about being overthrown
and often ordered investigation of political meetings by various splinter parties. There were hundreds of such parties in France at the time, only
a few of which advocated violent overthrow of
the government, but the men in office feared their
political power. There had been much protest,
both by party members and by the police ordered
to investigate, that the government's policy
violated civil rights. Therefore Vidocq's air of
apology for having to disturb Raoul on such a
matter was quite plausible.

"You won't find any bomb-throwing revolu-
tionists here," Raoul said with a grin. "You're
welcome to look."

"The report accuses you of printing and dis-
tributing certain revolutionary pamphlets and
songs," Vidocq said. "Frankly, the whole thing

is so silly, I didn't bother with a search warrant."

"You don't need one," Raoul said. "I have nothing to hide. Go ahead and search the place."

Vidocq searched the wine shop first, deliberately making the search perfunctory in order to convince Raoul that he was merely going through the motions to satisfy his superiors and that he wanted to get the matter over with as soon as possible. He was sure that any evidence, if there were any, would be in the living quarters upstairs.

Finished with the wine shop, the detective said, "Well, there doesn't seem to be anything here. I'll take a fast look upstairs and be on my way."

"All right," Raoul said agreeably, leading the way upstairs.

His good humor started to change to uneasiness when Vidocq started to search his living quarters, however. The detective's air of boredom vanished, and he went through the place with a fine-tooth comb. Too late Raoul realized he had been tricked and that this was no routine search for political pamphlets. But there was nothing he could do

since he had given permission for the search.

In a desk Vidocq turned up a bundle of papers. One was a summons whose cover sheet had been torn at one corner. Taking a scrap of paper from his pocket, Vidocq matched it to the tear. It fitted perfectly.

Jean Raoul stared at the piece of paper in the detective's hand, his face suddenly draining of color. Vidocq threw him an amiable smile, opened the attachè case and drew out the cast of a set of footprints. He was heading for the closet when Raoul decided to make a break.

Rushing toward a dresser, the man jerked open the top drawer. But Vidocq moved just as fast. The detective's hand closed in a powerful grip around Raoul's wrist before the man could lift the pistol from the drawer.

"You don't want to go around shooting policemen," Vidocq chided him. Then his tone turned formal. "Jean Raoul, you are under arrest for the robbery of Jules Fontaine."

Placing manacles on his prisoner, the detective

continued his search. In the closet was a pair of heavy shoes which matched the prints of the cast.

Vidocq now had plenty of evidence to convict the pair, but he always liked to build an airtight case. Jules Fontaine was brought to the jail and identified Raoul and Court as the men who had robbed him. They were also identified by the manager of the inn where they had dined with Fontaine. Other victims of robbery in that area were brought forward and also identified the bandits.

Georges Court, overwhelmed by the evidence against him, broke down and confessed to a whole series of robberies he and Jean Raoul had committed. Raoul held out longer, but he finally confessed, too.

Convicted on several counts of robbery with violence, both men received severe sentences.

But if it hadn't been for the remarkable mental file of François-Eugéne Vidocq, probably neither man would have been brought to justice.

This was one of Vidocq's last cases, for shortly

afterward he retired. He was one of the earliest criminologists to believe in the rehabilitation of criminals, and now he set out to practice this belief. He opened a paper mill and established the policy of employing only ex-convicts who had paid their debts to society and wanted to go straight. Many of these men he had hunted down himself, and now he devoted as much time to seeing that they kept on the straight and narrow path of honesty as he had once devoted to bringing them to justice.

Unfortunately the paper mill was not a financial success and eventually went out of business. However, it had given many an ex-convict the start he needed to become a useful member of society, and Vidocq worked tirelessly to relocate his employees in other jobs and continued to keep a watchful eye on them. Few drifted back into crime, although it is a debatable point as to whether this was the result of true reformation or because they didn't dare stray while under the relentless gaze of the famous detective.

The Boss's Case

John Edgar Hoover

The lean, curly-haired man who entered the Hot Springs police station that June day in 1935 had a face it would be hard to forget. His lips were so thin that his mouth was a bare slit, and he had the cold, unblinking eyes of a rodent. His face was deeply scarred in three places, one scar nearly four inches long.

"Dutch Akers in?" he asked the officer on desk duty.

Through the open door of his office Chief of Detectives Dutch Akers heard the question. Before the policeman could reply, he stepped to the office door to examine his visitor.

"My name's Ed King," the visitor announced,

115

extending a hand and looking the detective over as closely as the latter was inspecting him.

Dutch Akers was a hook-nosed man with a large Adam's apple which bobbed up and down when he talked. Six feet four and thin as a rail, he looked like a cartoon caricature of a country rube. But his small, deep-set eyes were shrewdly observant.

After shaking the stranger's hand, Akers said politely, "Excuse me a minute. I want to see if I have any mail."

He walked over to a mailbox on the wall. Directly over the mailbox was tacked a wanted poster bearing both front and side view pictures of a curly-haired man with cold eyes, a lipless mouth, and three facial scars. The poster said: WANTED FOR BANK ROBBERY AND KIDNAPING— FRANCIS ALVIN KARPAVICS, ALIAS ALVIN KARPIS. The detective studied the poster while pretending to search the box for mail addressed to him.

Turning from the mailbox, he said, "Come on in my office, Mr. King."

Inside the office, the chief of detectives shut the door. The man who called himself Ed King took a seat, drew a sheaf of bills from his pocket, and idly riffled them. Seating himself behind his desk, Dutch Akers glued his gaze to the bills.

"My brother Harold and I are vacationing here," the scar-faced man said. "We've rented Dyer's cottage at Carpenter's Dam on Lake Catherine. Plan to do a little fishing."

"Um," the detective said noncommittally, his eyes still on the money.

"We're both rather well-known businessmen, and people are always trying to get our autographs. I've heard the local cops are pretty good at keeping autograph hunters from bothering visiting celebrities."

"We try to make tourists' stays here as comfortable as possible," Dutch Akers said modestly.

"Here's a little expense money, so that the taxpayers can't accuse you of giving visitors special treatment at their expense," the scar-faced man said, laying the sheaf of currency on the desk.

Without comment the chief of detectives picked up the money and dropped it in a desk drawer. The scar-faced man rose to his feet.

"See you around," he said.

"Sure," the police officer said. "Drop in again."

Such was the way that Francis Alvin Karpavics, better known to the general public as Alvin Karpis, bought himself immunity from arrest in Hot Springs, Arkansas, at a time when he was listed from coast to coast as Public Enemy Num-

ber One. In the early 1930's Chief of Police Joe Wakelin, Chief of Detectives Dutch Akers, and other members of the Hot Springs Police Department grew rich by making the resort town a haven for wanted men. Among other noted citizens who poured bribes into their greedy hands from time to time for the privilege of hiding out from the law in Hot Springs were "Pretty Boy" Floyd, Elmer Farmer, "Lucky" Luciano, Harry Campbell, Frank Nash, George "Burrhead" Keady, and Sam Coker.

The "brother" whom Alvin Karpis told the chief of detectives was with him at the Lake Catherine cottage just outside of town was Fred Hunter, fellow bank robber.

That evening as the two bandits lolled around their rented cottage, Alvin Karpis on impulse decided to write a letter. He addressed it to J. Edgar Hoover, Director, Federal Bureau of Investigation, Washington, D. C.

It started, "Dear Mr. Hoover: I am going to kill you——"

Every boy and girl in America knows the name, J. Edgar Hoover. He is the symbol of honest law enforcement, the top G-man, the fearless and relentless foe of big-time crime—the cop who always gets his man.

This image is accurate, for J. Edgar Hoover *is* incorruptible, fearless, and relentless in his war on crime. But the mental picture it tends to create is that of a law officer who spends his time personally hunting gangsters and bandits, then capturing them at the point of a gun.

Hoover has done this on occasion, particularly in kidnaping cases where, whenever possible, he takes personal charge of investigations. But for the most part his work is administrative. Heading a force of more than six thousand special agents spread all over the country, he is usually as remote from the actual on-the-scene investigation of criminal cases as an army general is removed from front-line fighting. His great reputation rests primarily on his building the FBI into one of the finest law enforcement agencies in the world.

It is probable that his fights with Congress for proper laws and adequate money to make the FBI the efficient agency it is today have absorbed as much time as his fight against crime.

There are times, though, when Hoover personally takes command of investigations and personally makes arrests, even when the crimes are something other than kidnaping. This was what happened in the case of Alvin Karpis.

Alvin Karpis had been field commander of the ruthless Karpis-Barker gang, which under the guidance of the infamous "Ma" Barker had robbed at least fourteen banks and had kidnaped three persons for ransom. Shortly before Karpis' appearance in Hot Springs, Ma Barker and her only remaining son who was not either in prison or dead from police bullets died in a blazing machine gun battle with FBI agents.

It was this which enraged Karpis to the point of threatening J. Edgar Hoover's life. The bandit had adopted the bloodthirsty Ma Barker as a sort of foster mother, and he now decided he was going to avenge her death.

The effrontery of a wanted criminal threatening the director of the FBI was more than Hoover could take. It was not the threat to himself as an individual which angered him. He considered it an affront to the whole FBI.

Hoover accepted the challenge by issuing instructions that he was to be kept abreast of all developments in the Karpis case and that he would personally take charge the moment the man's whereabouts were discovered.

Unofficially Alvin Karpis came to be referred to by FBI agents as the "boss's case."

For nine months Alvin Karpis and Fred Hunter walked the streets of Hot Springs not as wanted men but as free as any law-abiding citizen. Their new Hudson car, bearing Ohio license plates, didn't even draw parking tickets from the friendly cops when they parked it in no-parking zones, for they were privileged visitors. Whenever money ran low, they hopped a plane to some other state, held up a bank, and returned with enough loot to buy further protection from the corrupt police and to live in their usual free-spending way.

The cottage the bandits had rented contained an old-fashioned icebox requiring the daily delivery of block ice. The iceman liked to read detective magazines. One evening in March of 1936, while reading one of his favorite magazines, he spotted the published photograph of Alvin Karpis and realized Karpis was the "Ed King" to whom he daily delivered ice at Dyer's cottage. He phoned the Hot Springs Police Station to report the man.

The next day the iceman told his employer what he had done. The employer, a little dubious about what action the local police might take, phoned the nearest FBI office in Little Rock.

The Little Rock agent in charge immediately started a group of special agents toward Carpenter's Dam to place the cottage under surveillance, then notified Hoover in Washington. The FBI director enplaned for Hot Springs.

While Hoover was en route to Hot Springs, the

FBI office at Little Rock got another phone call, this time from Chief of Detectives Dutch Akers.

"I have reason to believe Alvin Karpis is hiding out down here," the detective said. "Have one of your men drop in to see me."

The FBI was only too happy to oblige. When special agents called on Akers, he told them he had received a tip that "Ed King" might in reality be Alvin Karpis and that he had instructed his identification officer, Cecil Brock, to check up on the man's Ohio license plate. Brock, it developed, had wired the bureau of motor vehicles at Columbus, Ohio, and learned that the car was registered to an E. F. Parker of 323 North Phelps St., Youngstown, Ohio. Brock had then wired the Youngstown police and learned that the name E. F. Parker was unknown at that address.

Meantime the special agents sent to stake out the cottage learned that the birds had flown. When Hoover arrived in town he was greeted by this disappointing news.

Hoover listened to Dutch Akers' story with a

frigidness the chief of detectives found a little unnerving. When the FBI director asked why Akers hadn't immediately placed the cottage under surveillance when the iceman phoned in his tip, instead of merely instructing his identification officer to start shooting telegrams around the country, the detective could think of only a lame excuse.

"We wanted to establish first that it really was Karpis," he said.

How merely checking up on a license registration could accomplish this, Akers didn't explain.

The chief of detectives would have been even more unnerved if he could have heard Hoover's instructions to his agents after the interview.

"Karpis and Hunter have been hiding here for months," Hoover said. "At the very least it's highly coincidental that Akers didn't begin his flurry of investigation until after he knew Karpis had been identified by a private citizen who probably had also informed the FBI. I'd hate to think Karpis and Hunter were tipped off by a police officer, but I think we'd better make a quiet investigation of the entire Hot Springs Police Department."

These words were the beginning of the end for Hot Springs as a crooks' paradise. Harboring a fugitive from federal justice is a violation of federal law, which gave the FBI jurisdiction in the matter. Dutch Akers breathed a little easier when Hoover and his FBI men left town. What he didn't know was that different FBI agents immediately moved in and stayed. And once the investigation was begun, it didn't stop until Chief of Police Joe Wakelin, Chief of Detectives Dutch Akers, and Identification Officer Cecil Brock were all in a federal penitentiary for harboring fugitives from justice.

Meanwhile Karpis and Hunter had fled to New Orleans, disposed of their now-known Hudson, and bought a new car under assumed names. In the new car they took a vacation trip along the Gulf coast all the way to Miami, Florida, then doubled back again to New Orleans. Though they didn't know it, the FBI was only a jump behind them, barely missing them on several occasions.

Agents finally caught up with the pair in New Orleans. Hoover was in New York on April 30, 1936, when he received word that Karpis and Hunter were holed up in a Canal Street apartment in New Orleans and that FBI agents had the place staked out. He caught the next plane to New Orleans.

When he reached the New Orleans field office Hoover took command of the operation. Word came in from the agents staking out the apartment that the two men were still inside. The neighborhood in which the apartment was located had already been thoroughly surveyed, and all details of the apartment building had been noted. When this data was passed on to Hoover he gathered his men together for instructions.

On a FBI raid when the quarry is dangerous, every man has an exact assignment, and movements are timed to a split second. Hoover detailed men to cover the roof, fire escape, and rear entrance to the apartment building.

Then he said, "Three of you will accompany me through the main entrance to make the arrest. There is almost bound to be shooting because Karpis has bragged that he won't be taken alive. He is probably one of the most dangerous criminals we have ever come up against. I will not order any of you to accompany me, and it won't be held against you if you prefer a different assignment."

The three agents merely grinned at him.

"All right," the director said, grinning back. "Do any of you wish bullet-proof vests?"

Nobody did.

"Then let's go," Hoover said.

The raiding party left the FBI field office in two sedans, four men in each. They moved toward Canal Street at normal speed, obeying all traffic rules. As they neared the building the drivers were gratified to find a traffic lane open to the very front of the apartment house. Then, at the corner before the building, the traffic light suddenly changed to red.

Under instructions to approach the building as unobtrusively as possible, the drivers made no attempt to run the red light. The two cars quietly waited for it to turn green again.

As often happens in a raid, a complication developed. From the side street a mounted policeman on a big white horse turned in front of them just before the light changed. With a long stick tipped with chalk he began to mark the tires of parked cars. His slow-moving horse completely blocked the right-hand lane, which a moment before had been clear to the apartment house.

The FBI cars had no choice but to creep along behind the plodding horse.

When still a half block from the front of the building, the raiders saw two men emerge from the main entrance and move unhurriedly toward a black sedan parked at the curb.

"I guess we won't have to go in after them after all," Hoover said in a calm tone. "That's Karpis and Hunter." He drew his revolver.

The mounted policeman created a problem. There was the possibility that if shooting started, he might jump in on the wrong side, not realizing it was an FBI raid. Hoover made a quick decision and ordered that gunplay was to be avoided if at all possible.

The mounted policeman proved an advantage in one way. Alvin Karpis, who had slid under the wheel of the black sedan, had no desire to call even the casual attention of a traffic cop to himself. He had plenty of time to move away from the curb, which would have left the horse blocking the raiders from him, but he decided to let the horse pass first.

Hoover said to his driver, "When you come abreast of Karpis' car, stop."

"Yes, sir," the driver said, loosening his own pistol in its holster.

The two agents in the rear seat raised submachine guns from the floor onto their laps.

The white horse clopped on past the black sedan, but now Karpis had to wait for the two

cars trailing the horse to edge past. The front one halted directly alongside of him, the front door opened, and a square-faced man stepped out.

Alvin Karpis' jaw dropped when he recognized his arch enemy, J. Edgar Hoover. He started to whirl to grab a rifle from the rear seat but froze when he saw the gun muzzle looming at him.

"Get out, Karpis," Hoover said quietly.

Fred Hunter, seated alongside Karpis, started to reach for a gun, too, but he changed his mind when Assistant Director Earl Connelley suddenly appeared at the right car window with a leveled revolver. Both bandits raised their hands high overhead.

The raid had gone off smoothly and efficiently despite unexpected complications, but there was a comic anticlimax. Hoover, who enjoys a joke on himself more than one on someone else, still chuckles over it.

It developed that of the eight men in the raiding party, not a single one had brought along handcuffs! As a crowd gathered to watch the famed FBI in action the two bandits had to have their hands tied behind them with the neckties of some of the agents.

The comedy continued when the prisoners were put in the FBI car. Arrangements had been made to deliver them after arrest to the old post office.

When the director said to his driver, "You know where the post office building is?" the man said, "No, sir. I'm from Oklahoma and I've never been in New Orleans before in my life."

The two agents in the back seat were also Oklahomans who were totally unfamiliar with New Orleans.

Alvin Karpis, who hadn't opened his mouth until then, said, "Mr. Hoover, if you mean the new post office, I know where it is because I was just going to rob it."

Reminiscing about the case, J. Edgar Hoover says, "Fortunately for the dignity of the Federal Bureau of Investigation, it was the old post office where the prisoners were to be taken, and we didn't have to accept the proffered guidance. We did, however, have to ask the way of a passing pedestrian, who would probably have died of fright if he had known that the only thing between him and Alvin Karpis was an Oklahoma necktie."

At their subsequent trials Fred Hunter was sentenced to thirty years and Alvin Karpis was sent to Alcatraz for life.

Karpis was the last of the big-time bandits who for years had terrorized the country. John Dillinger, "Baby Face" Nelson, "Pretty Boy" Floyd, "Machine Gun" Kelly, "Ma" Barker, and others like them had all either fallen before the blazing FBI guns or were in federal prisons. This is a remarkable record when it is considered that the FBI had no power to move against these bandits until 1932, and in a mere four years it completely wiped out every major bandit gang in the country.

When J. Edgar Hoover took over the agency at the age of twenty-nine, the FBI was merely a fact-finding body with no power to make arrests and no authority to carry guns. Furthermore, it was staffed by men who had been politically appointed without much regard for their abilities.

With the backing of the attorney general, young Hoover made a thorough housecleaning, set the highest standards for his agents, and got Congress to pass a series of laws giving the agency some teeth. One of these laws gave agents the power to make arrests for federal offenses, another permitted them to carry guns. Other legislation made it a federal offense to rob any federal agency or bank where federal funds were on deposit, or attack or kill a federal officer (formerly this was only a violation of the law in the state where the crime occurred), or cross a state line to avoid arrest or to transport stolen goods.

With this new power Hoover declared war on the outlaw gangs who had been demonstrating their contempt for the law for years. And one by one he destroyed them.

When Alvin Karpis entered Alcatraz it was the end of a lawless era.

The Case of the Escape Artist

Francis Phillips

At eight o'clock one morning in 1929, the door-bell of a midtown Manhattan bank rang. The bank guard, the only one in the building at that hour, peered out to see a slim, dark-haired young man wearing a Western Union uniform. In one hand the messenger carried a briefcase, in the other a yellow telegram envelope. He held up the envelope to let the guard see it was addressed to the manager of the bank.

The guard opened the door, and the messenger stepped inside.

Handing over the yellow envelope and a receipt pad and pencil, the messenger said pleasantly, "Sign here, please."

As the guard's hands were occupied with the pencil and pad, the messenger calmly reached out and lifted the guard's gun from its holster. The guard stared blankly into the muzzle of his own gun for a moment, then slowly raised his hands.

The fake Western Union messenger reopened the door to let in another young man. As the messenger held the bank guard under his gun, the second man quickly lined up a row of chairs under the teller's windows.

Shortly after that the first bank employee arrived for work. At the instruction of the fake messenger the guard reluctantly opened the door to let him in.

As the teller stepped inside, he said, "Fine day, isn't it, Jim?"

"That's what you think," the guard said morosely.

Then the new arrival saw the men with the guns and his jaw dropped.

The man in the messenger's unform genially waved his gun toward the row of chairs. In a friendly voice he said, "Just have a seat, stay quiet, and you won't be hurt."

The teller took a seat and stayed quiet.

By eight thirty, eight employees were seated in a row facing the guns of the two robbers. The bank manager arrived last. He wasn't offered a seat. Instead, the man in Western Union uniform ushered him back to the vault and ordered him to open it.

Five minutes later, twenty-five minutes before the bank opened its doors to the public, the two robbers casually walked out the front door to mingle with and be lost in the morning rush of people hurrying to work. In the briefcase was $63,000 from the bank vault.

Although he had committed numerous burglaries prior to this and had already served time in two penitentiaries, this was the first bank job ever pulled by William Francis Sutton, who came to be known as "Willie the Actor." Willie got his nickname from the various roles he assumed during robberies: He appeared at different times as a Western Union boy, a fireman, policeman, and once as a window cleaner.

Willie's partner in this first job was Jack Bassett. During the next couple of years he and Bassett robbed banks and jewelry stores all over the east coast. When they robbed a jewelry store in midtown New York City of $130,000 worth of gems, Willie gained the distinction of being named the most wanted criminal in the United States.

By 1932 Willie the Actor was regarded as the dean of bank robbers. He had an extremely refined technique and always operated with two assistants. He never called them partners, for he made it clear that he was absolute boss on jobs and that the men he picked to help were subordinates. These assistants varied from job to job, but the two he used most often were Jack Bassett and an old friend named Eddie Wilson with whom he had grown up in Brooklyn.

His robberies were always carefully planned and always went off smoothly. Although he and his men used guns, never in a single instance was a victim shot or harmed in any other way. Willie never seemed very frightening with a gun in his hand, but there was a hypnotic quality about him which made people do exactly as he said without argument.

One bank manager's statement casts light on the peculiar effect Willie had on his victims. The man said, "I wasn't afraid for an instant that he might shoot me. As a matter of fact, I was sure I wasn't in the slightest danger. While his orders were definite, he never once raised his voice and he was extremely courteous. Yet I never even thought of trying to jump him, or of resisting in any way. There was just something about him that made you do as he said."

By 1932 Willie and his various assistants had committeed more than sixty big-time robberies involving a total loot of two million dollars.

A tip led police to Jack Bassett's wife, and through her Bassett was located and arrested in Buffalo, New York. Kitty Bassett wasn't arrested, the police preferring to leave her at large in the hope she would lead them to Sutton.

That is exactly what she did. One day detectives tailed her to a New York restaurant and closed in when she met a man there. The man was Willie Sutton.

At headquarters four detectives were assigned the job of questioning the notorious bank robber. They worked on him one at a time, attempting to get him to talk. Jack Bassett's confession had already implicated Sutton and himself in fourteen robberies, but there were many others the police wanted to know about.

One of the detectives assigned this job was a young member of the Main Office Squad of the Headquarters Force named Francis Phillips.

Today Inspector Frank Phillips—no one but his wife calls him Francis—heads the detective bureau which includes the automobile, forgery, and pickpocket squad; the safe, loft, and truck squad; the bureau of criminal information; the district attorney's office squad; the narcotics squad, and the bureau of special service and investigation. Only three people on the entire New York City police force are above him: the chief of detectives, the chief inspector, and the police commissioner.

Phillips started on the force as a rookie pounding a beat. He became a detective in a little more than a year and gradually worked his way up to his present position. He is widely recognized as one of the country's outstanding detectives. Over the years he has been instrumental in capturing scores of notorious criminals, but perhaps his most publicized feat was the case of the Willie Sutton gang.

The three other detectives had already finished questioning Sutton when Phillips took over. The young detective had had no part in the bank robber's capture, and to him this was merely a routine interrogation assignment. He had no idea that this first meeting foreshadowed a drama of prison escape, sleepless days and nights of police work for himself and other officers and, finally, a hair-raising chase ending in a gun battle.

The bank robber regarded Phillips wearily. "Cordes, McVeigh, and Lyons didn't get a thing out of me," he said. "Think you can?"

This was Frank Phillips' first look at the bank robber. Willie Sutton was not a very imposing figure. Thin and frail-looking, he had rather bulging eyes and a wide nose in a shrewd, thin-featured face.

Phillips said, "It's my job to try."

"You're Frank Phillips, aren't you?" the bandit asked.

Phillips was surprised, for as far as he knew Sutton had never laid eyes on him before. "How'd you know that?"

A secretive smile flitted across Sutton's face. "In my business it's just as important to case cops as it is to case banks. I could spot any detective on the force."

"I know a few things about you that aren't in your record, too," the detective told him. "As kids you and I lived a mile apart in Brooklyn."

It was the bandit's turn to be surprised. "No fooling? You lived around Prospect Park?"

"I used to play there every day. Probably we saw each other."

"Well, well. It's certainly a small world," Sutton said.

He visibly warmed, and they had a long chat about the old neighborhood and what had happened over the years to mutual acquaintances. Finally Phillips gently steered the conversation back to the subject of bank robbery.

Sutton grinned. "You're a smooth article, Frankie, but it won't work. Let's keep talking about old times."

Phillips grinned back. "Okay, Bill. I guess you're not going to loosen up."

As he rose to go Sutton said, "See you again, Frankie."

"I doubt it, Bill. Not where you're going."

Sutton smiled his secretive smile. "I won't be there long."

He wasn't. Both Sutton and Bassett were sent

to prison for thirty years. But in December of 1932 Willie Sutton slipped from his "escape proof" cell at Sing Sing, went over an "unscalable" thirty-five-foot wall, and disappeared.

Again Willie was listed as the nation's most wanted man, and every cop in the country was looking for him.

An informer's tip came into headquarters that Sutton was hiding out somewhere in New York City with his old helper Eddie Wilson. Every New York cop carried the two men's pictures and memorized their descriptions.

Then the Corn Exchange Bank on Broadway was held up by three men for thirty thousand dollars. The job had all the earmarks of Willie Sutton. A slim, dark-haired man with a soft voice had appeared in a policeman's uniform before the bank opened and had been let in by the unsuspecting guard. Covering the guard with a gun, the fake policeman then let in two assistants: a lean man with a deep voice who looked Swedish and a slim, good-looking Italian. The three robbers greeted and tied up fourteen bank employees as they arrived for work, emptied the vault, and leisurely walked out to disappear in the morning crowd.

Bank employees identified Willie Sutton and Eddie Wilson from pictures shown them at police headquarters, but they couldn't identify the third man.

Every known past associate of Sutton and Wilson was checked out. Relatives of the two men were kept under constant surveillance. But the bank robbers didn't go near anyone they had ever known. There wasn't a hint as to where they were hiding.

Then the Philadelphia Corn Exchange Bank was held up by the same three men. This time the leader wore a postman's uniform. The loot was $160,000, an impressive total.

On January 18, 1933, Captain Pat McVeigh of the Main Office Squad called into his office Frank Phillips, Dan Sheehy, Joe Arnold, Charles Beakey, and William Kirwan.

"You five men are relieved of all other duty in order to concentrate on a single assignment," he said.

"What's that?" Phillips asked.

"Bring in Willie Sutton."

Modern manhunts are no longer one-man affairs as they used to be in the days of the old West. Then they were relatively simple. The lawman tracked his man across open country, paused in small towns where every stranger was noticed to inquire if he had been seen, and eventually caught up with him in some frontier saloon where there was a gun showdown. The big cities have changed all that. Now a manhunt involves all the vast machinery of metropolitan forces. Victims have to be interviewed, informers' tips followed up, associates of the hunted men watched. A single officer couldn't possibly handle it all.

Frank Phillips was only one of five men assigned to the case, and he wasn't even the senior officer. A modest man, he denies contributing any more to the capture of the gang than any of the others. But according to his associates it was his brilliant police work and his suggestions for procedure which were largely responsible for the successful conclusion of the case.

The five detectives started by going to the police files on Willie Sutton and Eddie Wilson and memorizing everything in them. Then they sifted through the vast number of tips which had come in from informers, crackpots, and honest citizens who thought they had seen the bandits in various places. Splitting into two teams, they divided the tips up and started checking them out one at a time.

One of the tips was that Sutton and Wilson had recently been spotted in Jamaica, in the borough of Queens. Phillips, Arnold, and Sheehy drove there. They split up to visit every hotel in the area and show the bandits' pictures to desk clerks. One of the places Phillips visited was the Hotel Whitman.

The room clerk said, "That man was here last summer. He registered as Julian Loring." He pointed to the picture of Eddie Wilson.

Frank Phillips controlled his feeling of exultation. "Do you keep a record of outgoing phone calls?" he asked.

"Sure," the clerk said. He opened a record book and thumbed back to the previous August. "Here's a Canal number he called a dozen times."

He read off the number, and Phillips jotted it down. The clerk continued, "Then here's a Coney Island number. He asked us to get this one from information, so there's a note as to what it is. It's the Half Moon Hotel."

Phillips phoned headquarters to give the Canal number to Captain McVeigh to check with the telephone company. Then he rounded up his two partners. Minutes later they were on their way to Coney Island.

The Half Moon Hotel was an entirely respectable, upper-class place. The manager was a little upset when he recognized the picture of Willie Sutton as a former guest.

"The man seemed all right," he said. "In fact,

he really seemed quite refined."

"In a new suit you can't tell a bank robber from a preacher," Phillips said. "We're not suggesting that you deliberately harbored him. Do you keep a record of outgoing calls?"

"Certainly," the manager said.

There had been two calls to the Hotel Whitman in Jamaica. The Canal number was listed several times. Sheehy phoned headquarters to see if the number had been checked yet with the telephone company. It had.

"It's apartment twenty-three at two fifteen Chrystie Street," Captain McVeigh said. "The subscriber is a Charles Ingui. There's no record on him."

"Better get hold of Bill Kirwan and Charley Beakey and have them meet us near there," Sheehy said. He named a restaurant as the meeting place. "It'll take all five of us to check out the whole neighborhood."

The three detectives headed for Chrystie Street, where they met the two other officers. Until midnight all five drifted around the neighborhood singly, asking questions about the apartment house at 215 Chrystie. Charles Ingui had moved from apartment twenty-three, they learned, but hadn't bothered to have his phone disconnected. He had left it in for the new tenant, a slim, dark man named Joseph Perlango. Perlango lived there with his wife.

Phillips phoned Captain McVeigh to check Joseph Perlango's record; then the five detectives went back to headquarters. At two A.M. they had a conference in McVeigh's office.

"Looks like you've hit the jackpot," the captain said. "Perlango has a record of arrests for robbery, larceny, and theft. And he answers the description of the third bank robber."

"Shall we pull him in?" Arnold asked.

McVeigh shook his head. "We want Sutton and Wilson, too. I'll have a wire tap put on his phone. I want it covered twenty-four hours a day."

Today a court order is necessary before police can tap a phone. But in 1933 this wasn't required.

The tap was in effect the following morning. For the next eight days one or another of the five detectives sat in a cellar two blocks away with earphones on his head listening to every word said over the phone at apartment twenty-three, 215 Chrystie Street.

There were no important calls during the first seven days. Perlango phoned a few friends to invite them to a party on Sunday, the fourth of February. What incoming calls there were came mostly to his wife and didn't sound as though they had anything to do with bank robbery.

Then, on Saturday afternoon, the third of February, as Frank Phillips half-dozed with the earphones on his head, the phone at apartment twenty-three rang.

Perlango said, "Hello," and Phillips came wide awake when a deep, resonant voice said, "How are you, Joseph?"

The voice was that of Eddie Wilson.

"Fine, Eddie," Perlango said. "And you?"

"Perfect. Bill sends his regards."

Phillips motioned Arnold to start tracing the call. Arnold picked up a phone which was a direct line to Captain McVeigh's office.

"Any sign of heat?" Perlango asked.

"No. I'm planning to drive into New York tomorrow night."

"Are you crazy?" Perlango protested.

"Nobody'll notice me in all that traffic, Joseph. Nina's bored and wants to see some lights. I finally got my 1933 plates the other day, so I won't be stopped for driving with last year's."

"You went after them yourself?" Perlango said in a shocked voice.

"There wasn't any danger," Wilson said reassuringly. "I'm only five blocks from the city line. I scooted over and came right back. And, of course, I gave a fake name and address."

"You better stop taking chances like that," Perlango said dubiously. "Incidentally, I'm having a party tomorrow night. Sure wish you could be here."

Eddie Wilson laughed. "Not as hot as I am. The

three of us better stay apart. I'll see you."

He rang off.

In those days the equipment for tracing telephone calls wasn't as efficient as it is today. With modern electronic equipment a call can be traced instantly, but in 1933 a conversation had to last three minutes before the calling number could be traced.

Eddie Wilson had talked only two and a half minutes.

Arnold handed the direct phone to Phillips who repeated to Captain McVeigh the conversation he had just heard.

"Wilson said he was only five blocks from the city line," he told the captain. "That could be Yonkers. What would be the nearest branch office of the bureau of motor vehicles over that way?"

"Somewhere around Washington Heights," McVeigh said. "Wait until I check the book." There was the sound of riffling pages, then, "Broadway and one hundred and eighty-first. I'll give them a call. I'm sending Kirwan and Beakey over to relieve you. Come on in."

When Phillips and Arnold arrived at head-quarters, McVeigh had already received the necessary information from the branch office of the motor bureau. A man answering Eddie Wilson's description had registered a Chrysler sedan under the name of Kenneth Morley and had given a Brooklyn address. The address, of course, was fake, but they now had the license number of Wilson's car: 3-Y-2663.

"Maybe we can net him when he drives into town tonight," Phillips suggested.

"Just what I was thinking," McVeigh said. "From Yonkers the direct route is straight down Broadway, and he'll probably stick with the traffic so as to be less conspicuous. He won't risk it before dark, so be in position about seven. Phillips, you, Sheehy, and Arnold can set up at the city line. Beakey and Kirwan can set up a few blocks south, in case you miss."

At a quarter to seven that evening two un-marked police cars drove up Broadway toward upper Manhattan. Arnold drove the first with Phillips beside him and Sheehy in the back seat. Kirwan and Beakey were in the trailing car.

At 260th Street Kirwan and Beakey turned off, swung their car in a U-turn, and parked facing Broadway. Arnold continued on to 265th Street and exercised the same maneuver.

It was a bitterly cold night, and snow flurries lashed at what little traffic there was.

"There won't be many people out tonight," Arnold said. "We ought to spot him easy if he comes."

Phillips said, "Uh-huh," and Sheehy merely grunted.

An hour passed, then another. In the back seat Dan Sheehy held a flashlight to his watch. "Nine o'clock," he announced. "Looks like he changed his mind."

Joe Arnold gave Phillips an inquiring look. "What do you think, Frank?"

"Let's give it a while more," Phillips suggested.

By 10:30 P.M. even Philips was willing to give

up. Then, suddenly, he touched Arnold's arm. At the same instant Arnold and Sheehy said together, "There he is!"

The Chrysler sedan had just moved past the intersection at a moderate speed.

Arnold threw the car into gear and swung south on Broadway to follow it. Peering through the windshield, Phillips said, "That's the license, all right."

A girl sat beside the driver of the car ahead. The Chrysler moved along carefully, observing all traffic laws and hugging the right lane. Arnold began to inch over to the center of the street.

Some sixth sense warned the bank robber that it wasn't merely a pleasure car attempting to pass him. Suddenly the Chrysler zoomed ahead. Arnold drove the accelerator to the floor.

Luckily there was little traffic because of the weather, for the two cars raced down Broadway at speeds up to seventy miles an hour. Behind them Kirwan and Beakey had joined in the chase.

Gradually Arnold nosed the police car alongside Wilson's. Both Phillips and Sheehy had guns in their hands but they couldn't risk firing because of the girl in Wilson's car. Arnold started to pull ahead, planning to edge the other car over until it either had to stop or crash into them.

Wilson suddenly slammed on the brakes. But Arnold had been prepared for that maneuver and hit his brakes at almost the same instant. He swung diagonally in front of the Chrysler as he jolted the car to a halt, barely missing the front fender.

With one hand against the windshield to avoid being pitched through it, Phillips flung open the door and leaped out. He jumped on the Chrysler's running board on the driver's side as Sheehy raced around the car to the far side.

"Police officers, Wilson," Phillips snapped. "Throw up your hands."

The bandit's hands came up, but one of them held a gun. As the muzzle leveled at Phillips' chest, the detective squeezed the trigger of his own gun, aiming the gun upward so as not to

hit accidentally the girl or Sheehy on the other side.

The slug hit Wilson high in the forehead, plowing a furrow in his scalp but only dazing him. He slumped backward against the girl, and Phillips plucked the gun from his hand. Then Sheehy was climbing over the girl and pinning Wilson to the seat.

Moments later both the bank robber and the girl were handcuffed, and Phillips was giving first aid to Wilson's head wound.

"You've got a hard head," Phillips told the bandit companionably. "I guess you're going to be all right."

An ambulance was called, and Wilson was shipped off to the prison ward at Fordham Hospital. The girl, whose name was Nina Miranda, was sent to the women's section of the jail to be held for questioning. Meantime Captain McVeigh had arrived at the scene.

"Now let's hit Joe Perlango," he suggested.

At midnight Phillips walked into the apartment

house at 215 Chrystie Street, alongside Captain McVeigh. The building was surrounded. Phonograph music and gay laughter came from apartment twenty-three.

The door wasn't locked. The two officers walked in. About half a dozen couples were dancing. The dancing stopped suddenly, and someone turned off the phonograph. A slim, dark, good-looking man started to reach for his pocket.

"Don't try it, Joe," Captain McVeigh said mildly. "We're carrying guns, too, and the place is surrounded. You want to come quietly?"

The dark man looked uncertain for a moment, then slowly dropped his hands to his sides. "How'd you make me?" he asked.

"We've had you made for almost two weeks," Phillips told him cheerfully. "We were after bigger game. We just took Eddie Wilson. Now we'd like to take you downtown and talk about Bill Sutton."

Perlango looked stricken. "You got Eddie?"

"Uh-huh," McVeigh said. "Let's go."

At headquarters two hours of questioning failed to get anything at all out of Joe Perlango. Meantime Sheehy and Beakey drove to Yonkers and searched the apartments where Eddie Wilson and Nina Miranda had been living. At Wilson's place they found nothing of importance except a forty-five caliber automatic, but at Nina's they discovered a small black book with addresses and telephone numbers in it. When they brought the book back to headquarters McVeigh and Phillips were still questioning Perlango.

As Phillips thumbed through the book, Mc-Veigh said to Joe Perlango, "This is your last chance, Joe. Where's Willie Sutton?"

Perlango said sullenly, "I don't know. Last I heard he was in Trenton, but he's probably moved on by now."

In the book were a number of Trenton, New Jersey addresses and also several in Philadelphia. Phillips suspected that Perlango's mention of Trenton was meant to steer them away from where Sutton really was.

"Quit kidding around, Joe," he said. "We know Bill's in Philadelphia."

Perlango looked startled. "You do?"

"Sure. Let's quit wasting time, Captain. Joe doesn't want to make it easy on himself by co-operating. The address is right in this book."

Perlango stared at the book. "Did that little fool Nina write down the Chester Avenue address?"

Phillips grinned. "I'll have to check, Joe." He thumbed through the book, then said to Captain McVeigh, "Here it is. Forty-six nineteen Chester Avenue, Philadelphia. I guess that's it."

Perlango said in a crestfallen voice, "You tricked me."

"He's sneaky that way," McVeigh informed him cheerfully.

They drove to Philadelphia in two cars, Arnold driving one and Captain McVeigh the other. It was morning when they arrived, and by now all six officers had been up for twenty-four hours.

At police headquarters in Philadelphia they

contacted Chief of Detectives James Malone. Within fifteen minutes Malone had 4619 Chester Avenue surrounded. Malone, McVeigh, and Phillips went upstairs to apartment 207. The door was locked.

Backing across the hall, the three officers simultaneously threw their shoulders against the door. There was a splintering noise and it burst open. A slim, dark-haired man in shirt sleeves was standing in the front room. Giving them a startled look, he reached for a shoulder holster.

"Hold it, Bill!" Phillips said, leveling his gun at the man.

Willie Sutton hesitated, then raised his hands shoulder high.

"Hello, Frankie," he said in a weary voice. "I told you I'd be seeing you again."

In the apartment were three machine guns, six revolvers, some tear gas bombs, and a half dozen different uniforms, plus more than five thousand dollars in hundred dollar bills.

Willie Sutton went back to jail, but his career wasn't over even then. Prison managed to hold him for fourteen years, but on February 10, 1947, he finally managed to escape from "escape proof" Holmesburg Prison in Pennsylvania. This time he stayed at large for five years, not being recaptured until February of 1952.

At present Willie is number 12168 at Attica State Prison in New York. He has thirty years to serve, and when those are finished he owes 105 years for other crimes.

Willie is past fifty now and not as agile as he used to be. He is also watched night and day. It is unlikely he'll ever again make one of his miraculous escapes.

Still, you never know. When he was imprisoned the last time, he said to Frank Phillips, "I'll be seeing you again, Frankie."

Frank Phillips sometimes lies awake nights, wondering if someday he may have to do it all over again.

The Case of Fair Play

William Tilghman

It is hard to understand why the television industry has neglected "Uncle Billy" Tilghman. Television has glorified the lives of Wild Bill Hickok, Wyatt Earp, Bat Masterson, and Pat Garrett. All were formidable lawmen, but none even held a candle to Bill Tilghman.

For one thing, none of the others were career peace officers; they merely took occasional jobs as lawmen when there was nothing better to do at the moment. Hickok and Earp were basically professional gamblers; Masterson was a newspaperman; Garrett was a cowboy and later a rancher. Tilghman was a lawman at the same time as Earp, Masterson, and Garrett, but he had a greater reputation than any of them even then, and he was still a peace officer fifty years later, at the height of the Prohibition Era gang wars.

As marshal of Dodge City, Wyatt Earp kept the peace. But when he left, the town became as wild as ever. Bat Masterson kept the peace there, too, but the moment he moved on Dodge City reverted to its rip-roaring ways. Bill Tilghman took the job of town marshal, tamed Dodge City, and it stayed tamed. He arrested more badmen, broke up more outlaw bands, and cleaned up more bad towns than any other peace officer in the history of the West.

He even looked like a television hero. Tall, stalwart, and handsome, in the style of the legendary western hero. And he was utterly fearless.

Yet he was a quiet, gentle-spoken man who never bullied and never uttered a threat. Children followed him on the street, brought him their childish problems, and labeled him "Uncle Billy." He drew his gun always with regret, and only as a last resort. But when forced to draw it came out with incredible speed, and he could drive a nail at twenty paces. It was common in the early days of Tilghman's law enforcement career for aspiring young gunmen to pick fights deliberately with gunfighters of great reputation, hoping that by gunning them down their own reputations would grow. But even the most foolhardy young toughs avoided tangling with Bill Tilghman.

In his day Uncle Billy was regarded as the dean of all western lawmen, not only by the general public but by fellow peace officers. Wyatt Earp had profound respect for him. Bat Masterson once said, "It would take an encyclopedia to list Bill Tilghman's exploits."

In the mid-1890's Tilghman, already with a long career behind him as a town marshal and sheriff, was a United States marshal with headquarters at Guthrie, Oklahoma. He had two deputy marshals: Heck Thomas and Chris Madsen. In Oklahoma they were widely known as the "three guardsmen" because of their relentless hunting of criminals.

The three guardsmen were given the assignment of bringing the Doolin gang to justice.

Bill Doolin—tall, muscular, good-looking, with thick hair and a curling beard—had been a member of the Dalton brothers gang. When the Daltons were nearly wiped out in an unsuccessful double bank robbery attempt at Coffeyville, Kansas, Bill Doolin gathered the remnants of the gang together, enlisted some new recruits, and formed his own gang.

Before long the gang was the terror of Oklahoma. It held up banks, trains, and express offices, and even raided whole towns. Mothers frightened their children into obedience by warning, "Bill Doolin will get you if you're not good."

Even aside from the danger of the assignment, it was no easy task to track down the Doolin gang. The country was still rough and had many natural hiding places. Also, the leader had many friends among ranchers who engaged in rustling on the side, and the ranch houses of these men were always available for protection. Posses couldn't get near the elusive gang because the ranchers would pass on word of their coming from ranch to ranch until it reached Doolin long before the posses could get within miles of him.

Bill Tilghman decided the only way to get close to the gang was to move in alone. Since at that time there were nine known members of the outlaw band, all expert gunmen, this decision seems incredibly rash. But odds meant nothing to Uncle Billy. He would have gone even if the band had numbered one hundred.

One bitter January day in 1895, word came to Tilghman at Guthrie that the Doolin gang was holed up at the home of a rancher in the Rock Fort country. At the same time a complaint came in from another rancher accusing the Rock Fort man of stealing thirty-five head of his cattle. The U.S. marshal decided to visit the suspected ranch under the guise of inquiring about the rustled cattle.

Tilghman took a covered wagon loaded with camping supplies, and two riding horses tied on

behind. He went alone except for a half-breed
driver named Charlie Bearclaw.

It was a long trip across the winter prairie, and
a storm raged most of the way. Near dusk the
wagon came to a squatter's sod hut a few miles
from the ranch. Smoke was rising from the chim-
ney of the hut. It had stopped snowing and the
wind had died, but a dark sky threatened more
snow at any minute.

The marshal told his driver to pull up some fifty
yards from the sod building while he studied the
layout. No one was in sight, and there wasn't a
footprint in the foot-deep snow. This didn't mean
much, as the snow had just stopped falling, and
a hundred footprints could have been covered in
the past hour. However, there was no sign of
horses about either. A wooded area behind the
hut might have concealed horses, but it was a
good distance away.

"We might as well stop here to get warm before going on," Tilghman said. "I'll check the
place first. You wait here."

Leaving his rifle in the wagon, the marshal waded through snow the fifty yards to the door and knocked. When there was no answer, he opened the door and went in.

The building was one long room fitted out as a bunkhouse. Along either wall was a row of bunks with burlap curtains hanging in front of them. At the far end of the room a man hunched on the dirt floor before a roaring fireplace, his back to the fire so that he faced the door. He had a rifle across his crossed legs.

Moving forward, Tilghman said in a friendly voice, "Good evening. You mind if I warm up a bit?"

The man made no reply but he moved slightly to one side in order to make room at the fire. He was a stranger to Tilghman, but he was apparently the owner of the sod building.

Holding his numb hands toward the blaze, Tilghman asked, "How far am I from Bee Dunn's ranch?"

Gazing up surlily, the man merely shrugged.

A small warning signal sounded in the marshal's brain. In those lonely parts hospitality was
offered strangers as a matter of course. Normal
behavior would have been for the squatter to pour
his visitor a cup of coffee at once, then ask if he'd
like to eat. But this man hadn't even bothered to
say hello. And the rifle remained across his lap,
his finger near the trigger.

Silently Tilghman continued to toast his hands.
When they were thawed he calmly turned his back
to the fire. His expression remained serene and,
as he ran his gaze along the double row of bunks,
he didn't betray what he saw by so much as the
flicker of an eyelash.

The few windows in the building were too high
and too narrow to let in much light from the setting sun. The only other light came from the roaring fire. But it was enough to show an inch of gun
barrel protruding from the slits between the burlap curtains of every bunk—nine gun barrels in
all.

Tilghman knew then that he had stumbled

into the hide-out of the entire Doolin gang. He was a hairbreadth away from death.

Calmly he continued to bask before the fire as he considered the situation. There was no question in his mind that Doolin and the other eight hidden men knew who he was, for every outlaw in the territory knew his erect, stalwart figure. There was the factor, though, that Bill Doolin, despite his outlaw ways, was a stand-up fighter who scorned to shoot an enemy from ambush. It seemed quite likely that Doolin had recognized him as he approached the house and had ordered his men not to shoot unless the marshal made the first move.

On the other hand, they were a pretty trigger-happy bunch. Tilghman figured that Bill Dalton and Bitter Creek Newcomb would probably obey Doolin's order not to fire. But Little Bill Raidler and Little Dick West and Dynamite Dick Clifton wouldn't hesitate to shoot any lawman from ambush. Tulsa Jack Blake and Charley Pierce would prefer it to meeting him face-to-face. Red Buck

Waightman, so unpredictable that even his friends feared him, had sworn to kill Tilghman on sight. Any of these would interpret the marshal's slightest out-of-the-way move, even adjusting his hat, as justification to shoot.

It was an astonishing show of iron nerve that Tilghman could stand there and calmly reason out his chances in such a situation. But what he did next was even more amazing.

Though he wasn't foolish enough to push a showdown at such suicidal odds, Tilghman was so utterly without fear that he was incapable of backing away from a fight at any odds. With nine cocked pistols and a rifle trained on him, and his own gun beneath a buttoned jacket, he still decided to let Doolin know he was fully aware of his peril and wasn't even perturbed by it. He would make no overt move, and he would walk out if the bandits let him. But if they wanted a fight, they could have it.

In a calm voice he said to the squatter, "Reason I'm looking for the Dunn ranch is I heard Bill

Doolin is there. I've got a dog in my wagon I think can whip his."

The squatter said nothing.

"Well, I'd better be getting on," the marshal said carelessly. "If you see Bill, tell him I'll match my dog against his any time he's ready."

Without haste he moved toward the door, his hands hanging relaxed at his sides. The gun muzzles swung to follow him.

At the door he unhurriedly raised his right hand to the latch. Slowly he turned his head to throw an amiable smile over his shoulder.

"Thanks for the warm-up. So long."

The hunched man's eyes glittered at him, but he made no reply.

Tilghman opened the door, stepped outside, and closed it behind him. Eyes straight ahead, he plodded through the snow to the wagon, taking his time. He paused to kick the snow from his boots before climbing aboard.

"I guess you won't want to warm yourself in there, Charley," he said to the driver. "It's full of the Doolin gang. Drive on slow and don't look back."

As soon as the covered wagon topped a rise, Tilghman ordered Charley Bearclaw to stop. Grabbing his rifle, he swung from the wagon and waded back through the foot-deep snow to untie one of the riding horses which he mounted. From that height he could look over the top of the rise, and he saw a stream of horsemen ride from the woods behind the hut and pound off in the gathering dusk in the opposite direction.

Tilghman was then a half mile beyond the hut. Within minutes it would be pitch dark, and it was beginning to snow again. With a half-mile lead, tracks would be covered before he got back to the sod hut. Attempting to trail the gang in the dark would be a futile gesture.

It didn't occur to him that going after nine armed outlaws alone would also be a suicidal gesture. He gave up because he knew he'd never find their trail.

There would be another day, he told himself.

Returning to the sod hut, he found the squatter owner in a much more loquacious mood than at their first meeting. The man was only too eager to be co-operative. His behavior hadn't been by choice, he said. The Doolin gang had moved in and taken over his place by force. He had sat mute because he had been told he would be shot if he uttered a single word.

Tilghman doubted the man, but there wasn't much he could do about it except to continue to question him. The squatter denied any knowledge of where the gang had gone. But he did come up with one interesting piece of information.

"Bill Doolin saved your life," he offered. "The minute you pushed shut the door, Red Buck jumped out and ran for it, meaning to shoot you in the back. Bill grabbed him and pulled him back."

"Why?" the marshal asked curiously.

"Bill said you was too good a man to shoot in the back."

"Well," Tilghman said with raised brows, "I

guess I owe Bill Doolin a favor."

His lone attempt having failed, Bill Tilghman went back to the posse system to hunt the outlaws down. The three guardsmen, sometimes separately, sometimes together, led posses after the gang all over the state. Eventually things became so hot for the outlaws that they split up and ran in all directions.

Then, one by one, the three guardsmen ran them down.

The first to fall was Tulsa Jack, who tried to shoot it out with Chris Madsen. Bill Dalton shortly suffered the same fate by the same gun.

In March, killer Red Buck died shooting it out with a posse. Then Tilghman and Heck Thomas took Charley Pierce and Bitter Creek. In September Tilghman alone wounded and captured Little Bill in a duel at the Sam Moore ranch.

That left three members of the once-feared gang: Bill Doolin himself, Dynamite Dick and Little Dick West. They fled from Oklahoma.

But a United States marshal's jurisdiction

wasn't bounded by state lines. Through an intercepted letter, Tilghman learned that Bill Doolin was in Eureka Springs, Arkansas. The same night he stepped on a train for Eureka Springs. Hoping to take the bandit alive, he wore a long black coat and a high silk hat so that he might not be recognized instantly and have to shoot the man on sight.

The intercepted letter had indicated that Doolin was suffering from rheumatism and was in Eureka Springs for the health baths. Tilghman quietly went from bathhouse to bathhouse, lingering in the parlor of each for a time in the hope of spotting his quarry. Finally he walked into one where Bill Doolin sat in a corner where he could see everyone who entered.

Tilghman's unusual garb deceived the bandit long enough for the marshal to approach him and jerk out his gun.

"Hands overhead, Bill," Tilghman said pleasantly.

Doolin was a desperado, but he was a brave

one. Few men had the courage to face Bill Tilghman on equal terms. Bill Doolin made a try, even
with a gun pointed at him.

Leaping to his feet, he flashed his right hand
at a shoulder holster. Tilghman caught his wrist,
threw his shoulder into the man, and drove him
against the wall. His pistol bored into Doolin's
stomach.

"I don't want to kill you, Bill," the marshal said.

Staring into Tilghman's face, Doolin continued
trying to force his hand beneath his armpit, hook-
ing his left hand behind his elbow and pushing to
increase the leverage. Slowly but steadily his right
hand approached the gun butt.

Tilghman said in the same quiet voice, "I know
what you did at the sod hut, Bill. Let me do the
same for you. Don't make me pull the trigger."

Doolin only strained harder. His hand closed
over the gun butt under his arm.

"Good-bye, Bill," Tilghman said sadly.

But before he could squeeze the trigger, he suddenly felt Doolin's body relax. He released the

pressure of his finger just in time. Another split second and Bill Doolin would have been dead.

"Your six-full wins the pot," the bandit said laconically.

He made no further resistance when Tilghman took the revolver from beneath his arm.

This was not yet quite the end of Bill Doolin's career, however. He managed to escape from the prison to which he was committed. This time he was hunted down by Heck Thomas, who didn't go to as great pains as Tilghman did to avoid shooting outlaws. In a gun duel with Thomas, Doolin died.

There were now only two members of the Doolin gang still alive and at large. The next to go was Dynamite Dick, who had the misfortune to blunder into a restaurant where a posse had stopped for lunch. That left Little Dick West the only remaining member of the once-formidable Doolin gang.

But the relentless hunters finally found him. It was three years later however, on April 7, 1898, before Little Dick was tracked down. Bill Tilghman and Heck Thomas were together when the showdown came. Little Dick chose to fight, and he fell beneath Thomas' gun.

Bill Tilghman had been a law officer for twenty-four years when he and Heck Thomas dropped the last member of the Doolin gang, and he was destined to serve as a law officer for another twenty-six years after that. He was only twenty when he first pinned on a badge, and he was seventy when he died still wearing one.

Uncle Billy had retired when oil was struck at Cromwell, Oklahoma, in the early 1920's, and overnight Cromwell became a boom town. As always when sudden vast wealth gushes into a community, gamblers, sharpers, and thugs converged on the town from all over the country. The town became so wild and lawless that it couldn't keep a town marshal.

The city officials thought of Bill Tilghman and offered him the job. Against the advice of friends, he took it. The town toughs were gleeful at the thought of an "old man" attempting to tame them, but their joy quickly died. Though now seventy years old, Tilghman was as erect and steely-eyed and quick moving as ever. And just as tough. He tamed Cromwell as thoroughly and quickly as he had once tamed Dodge City as a young man. There was a steady exodus of crooked gamblers and sharpers who learned the hard way that the "old man" was no one to laugh at after all.

On November 1, 1924, a drunken prohibition agent named Wylie Lynn created a disturbance at a dance hall. Someone called for the marshal. When Tilghman arrived, Lynn began firing at his feet.

Tilghman would have been perfectly justified in drawing his gun and shooting the man dead, but, characteristically, he preferred to handle the matter without gunplay. Always reluctant to draw his gun, he was particularly averse to drawing against a fellow law officer. Calmly walking up to Lynn with bullets flying about his feet, he expertly and easily disarmed the man.

Taking Lynn by the elbow, Tilghman said quietly, "Let's take a walk over to my office until you simmer down, Wylie."

Lynn attempted to wrench his arm free, but he might as well have tried to pull it from a vise. Tilghman started to lead the man away as easily as though he were a recalcitrant baby.

It infuriated the prohibition agent to be so helpless in the grip of an "old man." Suddenly jerking a second gun from his belt, he fired point-blank.

Uncle Billy Tilghman, survivor of scores of gun battles with outlaws, fell mortally wounded by a fellow lawman.

The entire state of Oklahoma mourned the death of its most famous law officer. As flags throughout the state hung at half mast, Uncle Billy lay in state for three days at the capitol and thousands trooped past, hats in hands, to pay final tribute to a loved and respected citizen.

The Case of "Defend or Die"

William Campbell

The four best-known and most widely respected law enforcement agencies in the world are America's FBI, Britain's Scotland Yard, France's Sûreté Nationale, and Canada's Royal Canadian Mounted Police. The first three have already been discussed; a book on law enforcement officers, however, would hardly be complete without a chapter devoted to the Mounties.

It is difficult to pick a representative Mountie for a number of reasons. For one thing, the honor roll of red-coated heroes since the force was established in 1873 is so overwhelmingly large that any of hundreds of troopers could be singled out as outstanding law enforcement officers. A

187

second reason is that the R.C.M.P. has a policy of avoiding publicity for individual troopers. Like our own FBI, the R.C.M.P. never names the officer responsible for solving a crime when it issues a news release about the solution, with the result that there are no famous Mounties insofar as the general public is concerned. Names appear only in the official records. For a third reason, there are no Mounties famous for their individual techniques, because outside of such technical fields as fingerprinting and crime lab work, there are no specialists on the force. Unlike most police forces, troopers are not assigned permanently to a homicide division, robbery division, or similar grouping. Each trooper is expected to be thoroughly grounded in all phases of police work, and he may find himself one week assigned to a murder case, the next to a burglary, then perhaps to some traffic duty, and then be assigned to a remote outpost where he is the only law officer in an area covering hundreds of square miles.

There is not even a detective force as such.

Troopers are transferred back and forth from plain-clothes duty to uniform as needed, with no change in pay. A Mountie accepts without question any task assigned to him.

William Campbell has been picked as representative of the R.C.M.P. Many troopers, all equally anonymous to the public, have had as outstanding careers. Campbell has been chosen simply because he typifies the R.C.M.P. and the legend that the Mountie always gets his man.

When young Bill Campbell, fresh from recruit training, reported for duty to Fort McPherson, he was well-grounded in the various duties he might have to perform. Mountie training is unique in that it covers many things aside from law enforcement. This is necessary because a trooper may at any time be sent to some remote area where he is the sole representative of the government. He may have to act not only as a policeman, but as magistrate, postmaster, coroner, customs collector, government surveyor, immigration inspector, and tax collector. In addition he may have to issue licenses for dogs, cars, hunting, timber and mining claims; make weather reports; perform marriages; act as fire chief; and substitute for a doctor. The average Mountie is probably the best-rounded policeman in the world.

It was well that young Campbell had this background of varied training, for he was called on to use it at once. His very first assignment was a one-man patrol into the wilderness. He was ordered to pack a canoe with food, medical supplies, and winter equipment, and paddle down the Mackenzie River all the way to the delta. As winter was setting in and the river would freeze over before he started back, he was instructed to borrow a dog sled from Eskimos for the return trip. He was informed he would have no difficulty doing this as the Mounties were on excellent terms with all the Eskimos in the Mackenzie River delta region.

Campbell's duty was to check on all the people in the area. They consisted of three white men who were known to be trapping fur in the delta region, and several Eskimo bands. He was to check on the fur catch, report any births or deaths since the last patrol, and aid the natives and white trappers in any way possible. The trip would take weeks, and he would be entirely on his own.

As a final instruction his new commanding officer said casually, "Eskimos have reported two strange white men in the area who seem to have plenty of supplies and ammunition, but they aren't either trapping or prospecting. If you run into them, find out who they are and what they're up to."

The year was 1903, and young William Campbell was just twenty-three years old when he started out on this first assignment. He let his canoe drift down the river, using the paddle only to steer. Whenever he spotted an Eskimo camp, he beached the canoe and spent a day or two with the natives, gathering vital statistics, giving them what medical supplies they needed, and simply visiting. Finally he reached the delta.

Here the river split into many small streams

which cut into the flatlands in both directions. This area was full of silver fox. By searching out each stream, he located all three of the white trappers in widely separated places. Dutifully he counted their catches and inquired if they needed anything. In each case he left a supply of tobacco and a few medical supplies.

All three trappers reported having seen the two white strangers in the area, but none of them knew who they were. One impressed them as a city dude, the other as an old hand in the wilderness. They thought probably the dude was a rich sportsman and the other man was his guide.

Campbell moved on to the various Eskimo camps in the delta region. At one camp the natives said the two strangers had bought food from them and had stayed a few days. The greenhorn, whom they described as a nice, friendly man, was named Knute Johnson. The other, a big, surly man, was named John King.

Campbell spent a week searching for the two men, but although he found the remains of sev-

eral campfires, he never spotted the men themselves. Then winter struck and for ten days a blizzard roared across the delta. The temperature
dropped to seventy degrees below zero.

Campbell holed up in the igloo of an Eskimo
family and waited out the blizzard.

When it finally cleared, the river was frozen
solid. Leaving his canoe, the trooper borrowed a
dog sled and took up the search for the two mys-
terious strangers. At another Eskimo camp he finally caught up with one of them, Knute Johnson.

As the trappers had guessed, Knute Johnson
was a wealthy man who had come north to hunt
and had hired John King as a guide. The guide
had robbed him of all his money and supplies and
then abandoned him, Johnson said indignantly.
If it hadn't been for the friendly Eskimos, he
would have frozen to death.

"Who is this guide?" Campbell asked.

All Johnson knew about the man was that he
had hired him at Dawson City, five hundred miles
from there. "Can you get me back to civilization?"

he asked when he'd told his story.

"I'm not going there," the Mountie informed him. "I'm going after King. I'll have a rescue party sent for you when I finally get back to Fort McPherson. Meantime you'll be perfectly safe and comfortable here."

Campbell guessed that the renegade guide would head for Fort Resolution, which was really not a fort but merely an unoccupied stone hut which was kept supplied with food for hunters and Mounties on patrol. His guess was right. When he arrived the hut was empty, but ashes in the fireplace were still warm. He had barely missed the man.

The trail was easy to follow. It crossed the river and headed south through completely uninhabited country. Campbell headed his dog team in the same direction.

At dusk he reached the edge of a frozen lake. The trail was now so fresh that he knew the thief couldn't be far ahead, but he didn't want to blunder into him in darkness. He decided to halt in a stand of trees and wait for his quarry to give away his location by building a campfire.

When darkness became complete, a campfire flickered on the opposite shore, about two miles away. Staking his dogs and feeding them, Campbell set off across the lake on snowshoes.

Snow crackled under his snowshoes, for in the bitter cold the snow was as brittle as glass. As he neared the fire, he began moving each foot with infinite care. Fifty yards away he paused to study the scene. A huge, bearded man crouched before the fire.

Cautiously he started to move forward again, the crunch of brittle snow beneath his snowshoes sounding loud in his ears. He was within twenty-five yards when the man at the fire heard it, too.

Campbell knew by the man's swift reaction that he was a hardened criminal who must be wanted for crimes more serious than this last theft, for only really desperate men shoot first and ask questions afterward. Whirling, the man grabbed a rifle and shot in the direction of the

crunching he had heard. Almost in the same motion he leaped into the shadows beyond the circle of firelight.

The trooper reasoned that a man who reacted so quickly and violently would be an old hand at stalking his hunters. Undoubtedly he would circle in an attempt to get Campbell's silhouette between himself and the fire. Part of Campbell's training had covered just such a contingency. At full speed he backtracked a hundred yards, then waited.

His quarry didn't circle out quite far enough. After what seemed like hours to the young trooper, but was probably no more than ten minutes, the hulking figure appeared between him and the fire not twenty yards away.

"Freeze or I'll fire!" Campbell called.

The man stood rigid.

"Drop your gun," Campbell said crisply. He clicked his rifle bolt to add emphasis to the command.

The man let his rifle fall to the snow.

Moving forward, Campbell waved the man in the direction of the fire and stopped to pick up the dropped rifle. Back at the fire the two men examined each other. John King was well over six feet and probably weighed 250 pounds. Campbell, lean and wiry but weighing no more than 175 pounds, wondered how he would fare if the man made a break. Even though he was armed, a Mountie was supposed to shoot only to protect his life and was expected to handle recalcitrant prisoners without gunfire. If attacked he was limited to using his rifle as a club.

"Who are you?" King inquired sullenly. He must have suspected that Campbell was a Mountie, but there was no way of telling by his appearance. On winter patrol Mounties discarded their red jackets in favor of the fur parkas worn by whites and Eskimos alike in the Far North.

"I'm Constable Campbell of the Royal Canadian Mounted Police," the young trooper said. "You are under arrest for the robbery of Knute Johnson. I must warn you that anything you say—"

"Why, you young whippersnapper," King interrupted. "Think you can take me in alone?"

"I think so," Campbell said calmly. "Stand close to the fire and open your parka wide."

"Suppose I tell you to go to the devil?" King asked belligerently. "I know the Mountie rules. You can't shoot me."

"My superintendent is clear back at Fort McPherson," Campbell said cheerfully. "He can't see how I obey the rules. And nobody but wolves would ever find you out here. I'll give you about three seconds."

Actually Campbell had no intention of violating the rules, but the bluff worked. After gazing at him doubtfully for a moment, the big man moved closer to the fire and spread his parka wide. Campbell moved only close enough to see there was no pistol inside it, being careful not to get within range of those powerful hands.

"Okay," he told him. "You can button up again."

After ordering King to put out the campfire, he had him walk ahead back across the lake to where the dogs were tethered. He made the outlaw build another fire there, and they sat beside it until dawn. It was impossible for Campbell to go to sleep, for he knew the outlaw would jump him the moment he nodded. He did the next best thing. He kept the outlaw awake all night, too, by incessantly talking to him, so that in the morning King was no more rested and refreshed than he was.

The next day they trekked back to Fort Resolution, Campbell forcing the prisoner to move ahead and break the trail for the dogs while he guided the sled. This was routine procedure for bringing in a prisoner through snow. The man couldn't be shackled, for in the fifty-below-zero weather he would have frozen if unable to move freely. For the same reason he couldn't ride the sled. With both the trooper's hands busy guiding the sled, the only safe place for a prisoner was well ahead but within rifle range.

They reached Fort Resolution without incident and stopped for the night.

By now Campbell's every muscle ached for sleep, and there were five more days of travel ahead before they reached Fort McPherson. Inside the stone hut it would be safe to shackle the man without risk of his freezing, but that involved getting within reach of his powerful hands. Campbell had no choice but to stay awake again. Seated on the opposite side of the fireplace with his rifle across his knees, he eyed King steadily. But tonight he remained silent.

After a time what he hoped would happen did occur. The outlaw, as worn out as the trooper, dropped his head to his chest and began to snore. Quietly Campbell rose and tiptoed to him. With a sudden swoop he snapped on handcuffs and leaped back.

The outlaw awoke with a roar.

Ignoring the noise, Campbell picked up his rifle and stepped outside to the sled. He returned with a set of leg irons. King roared even louder, but with his hands shackled he couldn't put up much resistance. Campbell clicked the leg irons into place and chained him to a timber. Then he stretched out beyond the man's reach and went to sleep.

The next morning Campbell tossed King the keys and let him unshackle himself, then made him stand back while he collected the irons and placed them on the sled. After breakfast they started the five-day trip to Fort McPherson, King again in the lead breaking trail.

About noon they suddenly heard a baying in the distance behind them. King stopped dead in his tracks and turned a suddenly white face toward Campbell. The dogs stopped also, their heads turned in the direction of the baying, and they began to growl. Campbell felt the hair at the base of his neck rise.

"Wolves!" King said in a tense voice.

It was the most dreaded word in the Far North. There wolves moved in vast packs, and when hungry they would attack anything. Huge, gray, gaunt creatures, they were far more vicious and dangerous than either the gray wolf or timber wolf found in the United States, more closely resembling the terrible wolf packs of Siberia.

In the face of this danger the prisoner-captive relationship instantly dissolved.

Campbell said with a crisp calmness he was far from feeling, "Run for those woods just ahead, King, and get a fire going."

King didn't stop to argue. He headed for the woods as fast as his snowshoes would take him.

Campbell grabbed his rifle from the sled and turned to face the oncoming horde.

There must have been forty to fifty wolves in the pack—great shaggy beasts mad with hunger. At hundred-yard range Campbell took careful aim and dropped the leader.

Both his rifle and the one he had taken from King were only single-shot. He slammed home another shell, then saw his first shot had given him a period of respite. The pack, in its frenzy of hunger, had paused to tear apart its fallen comrade.

"Mush!" Campbell called to the dogs and headed for the woods where King was frantically gathering fallen branches and twigs.

The wolves had finished their feast by the time the sled reached the edge of the woods. Halting, Campbell dropped a second wolf, which succeeded in occupying the pack for another few minutes. Campbell drove the dogs on to where King was laying his fire and quickly unharnessed the team so that it could fight unhampered by the lines. Grabbing an ax from the sled, he tossed it to King.

"Give me my gun, Mountie!" King yelled.

"I'll do the shooting," Campbell said. "Get that fire going."

With a muttered curse King set flame to the tinder, then began to hack branches from a dead tree and pile them on the gradually growing fire. The five dogs stood with their fangs showing, facing the place the wolf pack was finishing the last of Campbell's second kill.

Then the pack started forward again, and this time it didn't stop to gorge on fallen brothers. Campbell fired as fast as he could reload, dropping a wolf with each shot, but still they rushed on.

Now they were within pistol range. Jerking out his revolver, Campbell dropped four more before the pack was upon them. Then, letting the pistol drop, so that it hung by its lanyard, banging against his leg, he grasped his rifle by the barrel and swung it as a club. All around him huskies

were fighting wolves, and out of the corners of his eyes he could see King ferociously swinging his ax.

The two men slowly backed to the blazing fire, swinging as they backed. When the flames began to singe their parkas Campbell gasped. "Faggots, King! Quick!"

Moving in front of the outlaw to protect him from the raging pack, Campbell continued to swing his rifle, batting wolves aside as fast as they came at him. King spun toward the fire, grabbed out a flaming branch, and hurled it into the center of the pack.

The beasts could face bullets, a clubbed rifle, and an ax, but they couldn't face fire. Howling, they backed away. King hurled more flaming sticks at them. The pack broke and raced to where their dead brothers lay and began ripping them apart.

Only one remained—a huge gray, who suddenly made a flank attack. Leaping on Campbell, he would have torn out his throat if it had not been for the heaviness of the clothes he wore. As it was, his fangs merely closed over fur. But the onslaught knocked the trooper down, causing him to drop the rifle. His hands gripped the wolf's throat.

There was a shot, the animal stiffened, then rolled lifelessly aside. Scrambling to his feet, Campbell saw King facing him with the rifle. The outlaw smiled grimly.

"We've saved each other's lives, Mountie. Want to call it quits?"

Campbell smiled just as grimly. Looking toward the wolf pack, he saw that its gorging was complete and it was moving off. Two of the five dogs were dead and the other three were wounded. With the reduced pulling power of the team, it would now probably take a week instead of four and a half more days to reach Fort McPherson. And he would have to stay awake the whole time, whereas his prisoner could afford to sleep.

Despite these overwhelming odds against him, Campbell didn't hesitate. "No deal, King," he replied. "You're still my prisoner."

King meaningfully hefted the rifle.

"It's single-shot," Campbell informed him. "And you just used its only bullet to kill the wolf." Raising his pistol, which still hung at his side by its lanyard and still contained two shells, he said, "Drop it, King."

Sullenly the outlaw dropped the rifle.

The next three days of the trip to Fort McPherson were a nightmare of hardship. Unable to risk sleep at night, Campbell dropped from exhaustion the third day on the trail. King took the sled, rifles, and the trooper's pistol, then left him lying in the snow. Fortunately Campbell revived before freezing to death and summoned a last ounce of energy to build a fire. Huddling by it, he got four hours of sleep, then grimly took up the outlaw's trail once more.

John King made two mistakes. He didn't search beneath Campbell's parka, where the trooper carried a second pistol, and he underestimated the Mountie's stamina. Assuming that Campbell would have frozen to death long ago, he made no attempt at haste.

Since the outlaw continued on in the direction of Fort McPherson, Campbell saw no point in rearresting him at once. Each night when he spotted King's campfire, he retreated far enough away for his own fire to be invisible to the outlaw, and got a night's sleep.

Twenty miles from Fort McPherson, William Campbell stepped into the outlaw's camp and rearrested him at gun point. King stared at him as though he were seeing a ghost.

"I couldn't let you get away," Campbell informed him cheerfully. "You're the first arrest I ever made."

"The first!" King exploded. "You mean I've been taken by a wet-eared rookie!"

The thought seemed to break his spirit, for he gave no more trouble. Once safe in jail at Fort McPherson, it was discovered he was wanted for a whole series of crimes throughout the Yukon.

But Campbell didn't learn of this for two days.

He spent the two days sleeping.

This was the first of many patrols William Campbell conducted during his long years of service with the Mounties. Although the general public heard little of him, he became a legend in the force for his ability to go anywhere in the worst kind of weather and always get his man. When he was a rookie the most famed trooper in the Yukon was Sergeant Dempster, who for many years headed the famous Arctic Patrol without ever losing a Mountie. Eventually Campbell was assigned to duty with this group, and when Dempster retired Campbell was made leader of the Arctic Patrol.

Sergeant William Campbell carried on the tradition Dempster had set. Although this famed patrol roamed the Yukon over thousands of square miles of territory, often hundreds of miles from any sign of civilization, through storms and blizzards which sometimes even killed Eskimos, Campbell always brought it safely through without ever losing a man under his command.

Whitman
CLASSICS

Five Little Peppers Midway

Freckles

Wild Animals I Have Known

Rebecca of Sunnybrook
  Farm

Alice in Wonderland

Mrs. Wiggs of the
  Cabbage Patch

Fifty Famous Fairy Tales

Rose in Bloom

Eight Cousins

Little Women

Little Men

Five Little Peppers and
  How They Grew

Robinson Crusoe

Treasure Island

Heidi

The Call of the Wild

Tom Sawyer

Beautiful Joe

Adventures of Sherlock Holmes

Here are some of the best-loved stories of all time.
Delightful ... intriguing ... never-to-be-forgotten
tales that you will read again and again. Start
your own home library of WHITMAN CLASSICS
so that you'll always have exciting books at your
finger tips.